EERIE AMERICA

TRAVEL GUIDE OF THE MACABRE

Designed by Matt Goodman
Type set in Times, Rosewood, URWWood,
Jivetalk & Gill Sans

ISBN: 978-0-7643-4469-5
Printed in China

Schiffer Books are available at special discounts for bulk
purchases for sales promotions or premiums. Special
editions, including personalized covers, corporate imprints,
and excerpts can be created in large quantities for special
needs. For more information contact the publisher:

Published by Schiffer Publishing, Ltd.
4880 Lower Valley Road
Atglen, PA 19310
Phone: (610) 593-1777; Fax: (610) 593-2002
E-mail: Info@schifferbooks.com.

For the largest selection of fine reference books on
this and related subjects, please visit our website
at www.schifferbooks.com.

We are always looking for people to write books on new
and related subjects. If you have an idea for a book,
please contact us at proposals@schifferbooks.com.

This book may be purchased from the publisher.
Please try your bookstore first.
You may write for a free catalog.

In Europe, Schiffer books are distributed by
Bushwood Books
6 Marksbury Ave.
Kew Gardens
Surrey TW9 4JF England
Phone: 44 (0) 20 8392 8585; Fax: 44 (0) 20 8392 9876
E-mail: info@bushwoodbooks.co.uk
Website: www.bushwoodbooks.co.uk

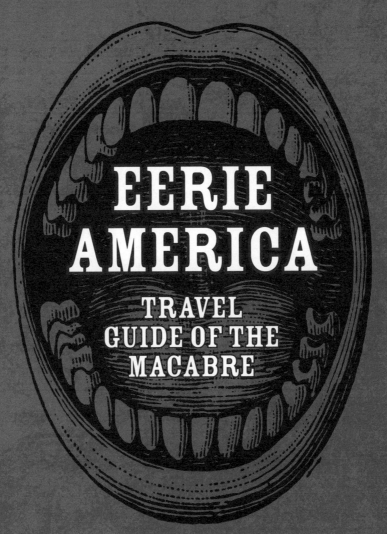

EERIE AMERICA

TRAVEL GUIDE OF THE MACABRE

E. R. "CORVIS NOCTURNUM" VERNOR
& KEVIN EADS, J.D.

Schiffer Publishing Ltd

4880 Lower Valley Road • Atglen, PA 19310

DEDICATIONS

E.R. Vernor would like to dedicate this book to those who paved the way in exploring what others have feared to understand.

Kevin Eads would like to dedicate this book to his mother, Patricia Kimmel, and brother, Dennis, for all of their support over the years, as well as his friends and fans for everything.

ACKNOWLEDGMENTS & SPECIAL THANKS

The authors would like to thank the following people, without whose efforts this book would not be possible: Mr. Pete Schiffer; our editor, Dinah Roseberry; Stacey McNutt in Marketing; Joanne Schioppi of The Discovery Science Channel; Mike and Evan of *Oddities*; The City of Colma; The City of Atchishon; The City of Saint Augustine; Leann, owner of The Lizzie Borden Bed and Breakfast; Eric Miller of The Mutter Museum; Ellen at Eastern State Penitentiary; Lindsey Huffman, Marketing Coordinator for Winchester Mystery House; Vickie Carson, Public Information Officer at the Mammoth Cave; Cherryl Kaopua, Senior Public Relations Manager of the Hard Rock Café; Danielle at The Museum of the Weird; Cortlandt Hull of The Witches Dungeon; Tina Jordon of The Witchcraft Museum; Myles Ollen of Bowlin Travel for The Thing?; Angie Green, Director of Save Our Cemeteries and Lafayette Cemetery No. 1.; Kathy Reno, St. Joseph Museums, Inc. of The Glore Museum; Carol Lee of The USS *Hornet* Museum; Eleanor Cunningham, Director of The Gaineswood Plantation; Kenneth Drumm of the Otesaga Resort Hotel; Skot Jorz, Office of Public Affairs National Parks; the Montana Historic Society, and the countless others who provided images and commentary for this book.

Special thanks to Sarah Imholte, the PR Coordinator for the Science Museum of Minnesota where Questionable Medical Devices currently are on display, as well as the provided images and details.

We thank you for your assistance and enthusiasm.

CONTENTS

INTRODUCTION . . . 11

AUTHOR NOTE

IT IS ADVISABLE TO ALWAYS EITHER CALL AHEAD OR RESEARCH A PLACE'S WEBSITE BEFORE PLANNING A VISIT TO CHECK TIMES, FEES, AND OTHER PERTINENT FACTS. VISITOR INFORMATION HERE WAS CORRECT AT TIME OF PRINTING BUT COULD BE SUBJECT TO CHANGE AT ANY TIME PER EACH LOCATION'S AVAILABILITY.

INTRODUCTION

Reflecting back on how the concept of this book began is both a walk down memory lane and my own desire to explore other wonders detailed here firsthand. It began a few years ago when I visited Philadelphia to participate in an art gallery showing at the now-closed Germ Gallery, a bookstore for the strange and unusual. While there, I passed the infamous East State Penn, as it is called, whose foreboding size and history is the stuff of documentaries, not to mention a ghost hunter's delight. I knew tours were given there, and as I continued along my trek through one of America's oldest cities, I discovered an even more unique place, The Mütter Museum. This was a thrill for me as I had never been in such a place. Not only was it creepy, in a way, but highly educational as well. As I listened to the tour guide, I asked myself, "What other odd places are in the United States? Surely there are many others like this." I overheard someone mention with a laugh that it reminded them of The Edgar Allen Poe Museum. I reflected back on this as I went on to write other books, and I couldn't get the idea of writing a book about such places out of my head.

While I attended college, my now colleague, Professor Kevin Eads (a law professor who is a lover of television shows dealing with hauntings and a horror buff, as well) was in the middle of a lecture on the importance of note taking. He made a joke to lighten up the academic monotony by referencing Elizabeth Bathory, a Hungarian countess known for torturing women for fun.

In the beginning, Kevin knew me as his student, Eric Vernor, but later learned of my books under the pen name of Corvis Nocturnum. We hit it off after class and I told him my idea for this book. He was instantly intrigued with the idea and expressed his interest in lending a hand. I was delighted, seeing as taking on all fifty states was such a daunting task and would have taken me so much time, it was good to get some assistance.

Through the next couple months, into the following year, we researched, compared notes, and got together to add more and more to it. The idea to add in the traveling aspects was Kevin's suggestion, as he moonlighted at a hotel as a night auditor, and joked about The Lizzie Borden Bed and Breakfast. This is what inspired the comprehensive list of places to wine and dine where there was an unusual story involved so that readers could treat themselves to thrills and chills along the way.

Eerie America: Travel Guide of the Macabre could very well be called *The Fodor's Travel Guidebook for The Addams Family* as you, the reader, will find some of the most macabre, haunted, and bizarre places located all over the United States. You will see glimpses of places like Discovery Channel's *Oddities* show, as well as many other locations that do indeed give guided tours and have offered comments and provided amazing photographs.

The purpose of this book is to entertain you and to give you a glimpse of places you never knew existed. With the cooperation of many city and state museums, we are making an effort to promote tourism for some fascinating and unusual locations around the United States...and to provide a history lesson to readers. Our wish is to educate people regarding the richness that can be found within the U.S.—all people have to do is seek it out. Or, if you are feeling especially adventurous and dare to visit these places for yourself, we have added several establishments where you can stay overnight and/or dine as you make the trip around the country!

This is the first book ever geared toward dark tourism—that is to say, places of oddities, curiosities, the strange, the bizarre, and the beautiful. Follow us as we visit the fifty states, walk famous cemeteries with haunting reputations, climb through ghostly old battleships, journey through abandoned prisons and creepy lunatic asylums, stroll the corridors of eerie museums, and call upon famous haunted houses and other bizarre places that you might never have realized were in your own backyard.

—E.R. Vernor

*Sloss Furnaces
Birmingham.
Photograph courtesy
Library of Congress*

ALABAMA

*** WHERE TO VISIT ***

BIRMINGHAM, SLOSS FURNACE

The Sloss Furnace, in Birmingham, is considered to be one of the scariest places in Alabama. In the year of 1882, this industrial business began processing coal and various types of ore into steel.

James Withers Sloss constructed the various furnaces known as the Sloss Furnace. Completed in 1881, it was referred to as "City Furnaces." The workers had to do their jobs in severe conditions, with high temperatures and other dangers that resulted in hundreds of men dying while working at this facility.

One of the hauntings that people report at the Sloss Furnace is of a man by the name of Theophilus Jowers. He was extremely proud to be a part of the iron industry and often bragged to his wife and friends that the furnace was his "friend." Unfortunately, he slipped and actually fell *into* one of the furnaces, thus putting an end to his annoying the crew!

There are also several other hauntings that are said to occur at this facility, like old Mr. Jowers who meets his demise in the furnace. Visitor's say they see him walking the catwalks. Also, the ghost of James Wormwood, who died by in taking methane gas and falling into the highest furnace (called "Big Alice") has been seen.

SLOSS FURNACES NATIONAL HISTORIC LANDMARK
Twenty 32nd Street North, Birmingham, AL 35222 Phone: (205) 324-1911

Admission is free. Tuesday through Friday 10 a.m. to 4 p.m.

GAINESWOOD PLANTATION

The Gaineswood Plantation was designed by the owner, General Nathan Whitfield, and was constructed between 1843-1861, with much of the work being done by slaves, freedmen, and artisans, such as painter John Verdin.

Gaineswood is considered to be one of the finest neoclassical houses in the U.S. and one of the few that uses Doric, Ionic, and Corinthian, the three ancient Greek architectural orders.

The current museum contains original family furnishings and the grounds also feature a gatehouse, gazebo, plantation office, and a pantry.

I spoke to the director, Eleanor Cunningham, about the alleged paranormal occurrences at the location. The official record of the plantation site is that there are no occurrences of paranormal activity.

But, some time ago, Katherine Tucker Windham in her book *13 Alabama Ghosts and Jeffrey* told tales of the ghost of Evelyn Carter, who died at Gaineswood while visiting her sister, who was housekeeper. Originally from Virginia, she wanted to be buried back home, but due to a bad winter, her body was stored in the basement. According to the legends, her spirit was said to have never left the house and that footsteps on the guest stairways can be heard.

Gaineswood staff is happy to share "The Facts Behind the Fiction," a short presentation highlighting the real occurrences that gave rise to the popular ghost story. Despite the alleged tales, the rich history of the place itself and the beautiful grounds is more than enough to bring countless tourists to Gaineswood National Historic Landmark.

Regardless if you have a close encounter with her ghost or any other, you cannot miss a chance to see such a divine piece of classical architecture in the Deep South.

GAINESWOOD PLANTATION

805 South Cedar Avenue, Demopolis, AL 36732 Phone: (334) 289-4846 Website: www.preservela.org

Gaineswood is currently open Tuesday through Friday 10 a.m.- 4 p.m.; the first Saturday of the month
10 a.m.-2 p.m.; and other times by appointment. Gaineswood observes all state holidays.

★ WHERE TO EAT ★ ★ WHERE TO STAY ★

JACK'S RESTAURANT

THE RAWLS HOTEL

It is said that something scary happens almost every day at Jack's Restaurant. Their story comes from an Indian ghost who they call Mary. She is alleged to throw things from the shelves, open the doors to the oven, and then slam them closed. There are also stories that the night crew has turned off the grills, and in the morning, the grills are turned back on. (Just imagine the electric bills off of that.) It is said that there is not a day that passes that the workers don't find something disturbing that has occurred.

So, enjoy some great food, and maybe have a ghost whisper in your ear to give you tips about what you should order.

JACK'S RESTAURANT
6258 Highway 269
Parrish, AL 35580
Phone: (205) 686-5863
Website: www.eatatjacks.com

The Rawls Hotel was founded in 1903 and includes a lounge, a bed and breakfast, and the Rawls Restaurant, where you can enjoy fine dining.

The hotel's website is also quick to point out the alleged hauntings at the famous landmark. It states that there are many unusual occurrences here.

People hear children's laughter from the third floor when there are no children around. Many people have claimed to have seen apparitions on the second and third floor. It is not at all uncommon to hear the sounds of doors opening and closing and footsteps on these floors when no one is there to account for the noise.

The hotel's website includes a diary-style article from a reporter who spent the night and the paranormal experiences she had throughout that night.

So, come and spend the night or enjoy a fine dinner. You never know what you might experience.

RAWLS HOTEL
116 S. Main Street, Enterprise, AL
Phone: (334) 347-7612 Website: http://www.rawlsbandb.com

The Rawls Hotel is located in downtown Enterprise, Alabama and is only a block away from the Boll Weevil Monument, which you must visit while in town.

ALASKA

WHERE TO STAY

★ ★ ★   ★ ★ ★

THE GOLDEN NORTH HOTEL

The Golden North Hotel in Skagway is rumored to be a haunted hotel. Built in the year of 1898, and moved to its current location in 1908, another story was added to the top in an effort to bring it to three stories instead of two, as well as a golden dome.

The most popular haunting that is said to reside in the hotel is that of a spirit called "Mary." Back during the early days of prospecting for gold, Mary's fiancé, doing well in the business, reserved a room for her at the hotel. He left her there to go back to prospecting, and while he was away, she developed pneumonia and died.

To this day, guests claim to see the spirit of Mary in her old room, Number 23, and report they wake up feeling as if they are choking. Odd lights are reported in other parts of the hotel as well.

If you wander up into this beautiful part of the country, be sure and reserve a room to see for yourself!

THE GOLDEN NORTH HOTEL
3rd & Broadway
Skagway, AK
Phone: (907) 983-2451
Website: http:// www.goldennorthmotel.com

ARIZONA

WHERE TO VISIT

★ ★ ★ ★ ★ ★

THE THING? WHAT IS IT?

On vacation a few years back, my brother and I were traveling through New Mexico and Arizona, and signs would keep popping up for an attraction called "The Thing? What Is It?" Being that we are curious travelers, we wanted to stop by before visiting a friend later that evening in Tucson.

I believe that we paid one dollar to enter the attraction. We walked through the many exhibits along the way. There was a covered wagon and many automobiles, including a Rolls Royce they claim belonged to Adolf Hitler, and a host of other interesting exhibits. At the end, you come to *The Thing?* So, what is it? You will have to make the visit to find out, and while there, be sure to visit the one-of-a-kind gift shop for all sorts of unique gifts.

THE THING? WHAT IS IT?
2631 North Johnson Road, Dragoon, AZ 85609
Phone: (520) 586-2581

Directions: I-10 exit 322, south side. Hours: daily 6:30 a.m. until dark. (Call to verify)
Admission: Adults $1, 6-18 $.75, Under 6 free. Owned by the Bowlin Travel Center, The company
is over a hundred years old and has other locations in southern Arizona and New Mexico!

THE
BIRD CAGE THEATRE

Take a trip back in time to one of the wildest places around in the 1880s Old West. The Bird Cage Theatre served not only as a theatre, but a saloon, gambling hall, and place where the "ladies of the night" would entertain gentlemen for the right price. The prostitutes would actually entice clients from within fourteen red velvet-draped cages that hung from the ceiling, which in and of itself could be considered a fascinating concept.

The structure has been rumored to have a past that is quite violent. It is said that between the years 1881 and 1889, the Bird Cage Theatre was home to at least twenty-six murders and during those eight years, it was considered one of the wildest places in the West. In 1889, it closed and was boarded up. It was reopened in 1934, by the Hunley family, in its original state, bringing in tourists.

The theatre has Doc Holliday's faro table, the game he most enjoyed playing. Also, Tombstone's original Boothill hearse, the Black Mariah, is on display in the theatre. It is one of only eight made back in the 1880s.

Visitors and employees of the theatre have reported seeing the ghosts of cowboys and prostitutes. There have been reports at night of the sounds of laughter, music, and yelling coming from different parts of the building. Some people have claimed to have been pushed or touched, but seeing no one around to do so.

The Hunley family turned the theatre into an attraction that would allow tourists to experience the history of the building, as well as the town of Tombstone. This increased the popularity of the theater dramatically. Ghost hunters, societies that worked to uncover the mysteries behind paranormal events, and even the media literally swarmed the building at every opportunity in order to catch a glimpse of one of the spirits that were said to haunt the building, or experience some of the unexplained phenomenon that was rumored to occur at the establishment.

The owners are thrilled when someone reports a haunting or an event that could be attested to the supernatural, and they have been featured on a few television shows, where the owner said the most active period for the establishment happens after about nine in the evening, each evening.

The theatre is not only a hotspot for paranormal activity, but a must-see stop for any tourist passing through Arizona.

THE BIRD CAGE THEATRE
517 East Allen Street, Tombstone, AZ 85638
Phone: (520) 457-3421 Website: http://tombstonebirdcage.com

Ghost tours are available daily at the Bird Cage Theater, in the town of Tombstone. Bring your camera,
comfortable walking shoes, and a sense of adventure to the most infamous saloon in the town that never dies.

YUMA
TERRITORIAL PRISON

The Arizona Territory's first prison opened July 1, 1876, and the first seven prisoners actually helped to build it. The prison is now a museum and shows exhibits of prison life and what it was like to be incarcerated. It has a gift shop for tourists as well.

The evidence shows that the prison was administered in a humane manner and was a model prison during its thirty-three years of operation. The major punishments were the ball and chain for those who tried to break out and dark cells for those who had broken regulations. The prisoners had free time when many would hand-craft items, which would be sold at the public bazaar held at the prison on Sundays.

Over 100 prisoners were said to have died during their stay at the prison, and many are said to still haunt this fortress. The hauntings are said to be strongest in the dark cell. Park rangers and staff members have spoken about strange occurrences there. But it is not just the dark room that is said to be haunted, the offices and the museum have also had their own strange occurrences. Things are often moved and lights will go on and off. It was reported that, on one occasion, coins from the cash register in the gift shop flew into the air and landed back in the drawer.

This is a great place to visit, not only for a ghostly adventure, but to get a feel for what life would really be like for an outlaw in the Old West when they were finally caught.

YUMA TERRITORIAL PRISON
1 Prison Hill Road, Yuma, AZ 85264
Phone: (928) 783-4771 Website: http://www.yumaprison.org/index.html

It closed in 1910 due to overcrowding, but opened again, in 1961, to the public for viewing.
You can walk into the cells, climb high into the guard tower, and shop for novelties in the gift shop.
From June 1 to September 30, the park will be open 9 a.m. to 5 p.m., and closed on Tuesdays and Wednesdays.
Check for updated times before visiting.

WHERE TO EAT

BIG NOSE KATE'S SALOON

When many people think of Tombstone, they think of the OK Corral, which I understand. Tombstone is a city rich in history of another time and era. We imagine the old cowboy movies our grandfathers probably watched with us when we visited as kids. There is much of this here, but there is another side, a haunted side.

The building itself was opened in 1881 as the Grand Hotel, a high-class place with fine dining and plenty of beer flowing. It was well known, not only with the locals, but with those traveling. The place was later named for Big Nose Kate (Mary Katharine Harmony), a former prostitute, who is famous for allegedly busting Doc Holliday out of jail. They are said to have had a relationship over the years, living together, but never getting married.

It is said that the Clantons and the McLaurys stayed at this establishment the night before they were killed at the shootout at the OK Corral.

One spirit that is said to haunt the establishment is named Felix. He is said to be dressed in 1880s attire and roams the hallways. Some accuse him of pinching the waitresses and calling out people's names. A female spirit dressed in 1880s attire is seen at times at the balcony listening to the music. Glasses at the tables and at the bar are said to move by themselves. Doors and cupboards open without assistance. People hear voices coming from the basement when no one is there. Patrons experience cold spots.

So, when you pull into Tombstone, grab a table at Big Nose Kate's, enjoy some excellent food and a beer—you never know what the entertainment may be that night.

BIG NOSE KATE'S SALOON
417 East Allen Street, Tombstone, AZ 85638
Phone: (520) 457-3107 Website: www.bignosekates.info

Gadsden Hotel. *Photograph courtesy Robin Brekhus and David MacDougal*

THE JEROME GRAND HOTEL

The Jerome Grand Hotel was originally built as a hospital in 1927, and, by 1930, was considered one of the best equipped in the western states. It was built in the Spanish Mission Style of architecture. The hospital closed in 1950 and the building was unused until 1994, when they began to renovate the building, and the hotel opened in 1997.

The hotel itself seems to embrace the alleged hauntings that occur in the structure. There are unexplained smells of flowers, cigarettes, and whiskey, and people talk of strange sounds coming from empty rooms, such as coughing and voices. There are said to be two female specters seen by many visitors. One is a nurse with a clipboard who roams the halls checking in on her patients. The other is a woman in white who is said to have died giving birth. Allegedly, her dead child was buried in an unmarked grave and she stalks the place looking for the burial spot.

The hotel puts on ghost hunts, which are quite extraordinary for such an establishment. While many places like to keep their hauntings quiet, the Jerome not only embraces the hauntings, but seems to celebrate them.

THE JEROME GRAND HOTEL
P.O. Box H, 200 Hill Street, Jerome, AZ 86331
Phone: (928) 634-8200 Website: www.jeromegrandhotel.net/

The Award Winning Asylum Restaurant is located one floor above the lobby level and offers lunch and dinner every day. The Owners of the Asylum Restaurant are proud to be recipients of the award of excellence from *Wine Spectator* magazine. They can accommodate private parties and small groups.

THE GADSDEN HOTEL IN DOUGLAS

The Gadsden Hotel in Douglas is a remarkable piece of architecture. The hotel opened in 1927, when Arizona was still a territory. The hotel burned down in 1929, but was rebuilt. In 1988, after years of neglect, it was taken over and has been restored to glory. Dignitaries and celebrities have stayed in the hotel, and there have even been movie shoots held there.

Many talk about the famous Gadsden Ghost who roams the hallways. Those who work at the hotel and guests have reported that Lent and Christmas seem to be a time when a ghost is often seen in the basement.

The hotel also has fine dining available. If you are tired from your trip out west and need a place to dine and rest, be sure to make the Gadsden a stop on your tour.

THE GADSDEN HOTEL IN DOUGLAS
1046 G Avenue, Douglas, AZ 85607
Phone: (520) 364-4481
Website: www.hotelgadsden.com/hotel.html

Gadsden Hotel. *Photograph courtesy Robin Brekhus and David MacDougal*

THE
COPPER QUEEN HOTEL

A stay at the Copper Queen Hotel is like stepping back to another era. The building was completed in 1902. It was built by the Phelps Dodge Mining Company as a place for investors and dignitaries to have a luxurious place to stay while in Bisbee.

The hotel was built in an Italian style with mosaic tile from Italy installed throughout the first floor lobby and the hotel lobby. Construction was not easy. Phelps Dodge had to blast away and clear a large portion of the mountainside to even begin. It was one of the most modern hotels in the west when it began, but there have been many changes that will make your experience even better.

The Copper Queen Hotel is quick to point out their best asset: the ghosts that haunt the building. I am sure that you, much like I, truly enjoy a hotel that sells this aspect of their business rather than hiding it. On their website, they talk not only about the particular ghosts you will find in the hotel, but also the fact that the popular television series *Ghost Hunters* filmed an episode here.

The first ghost is said to be an older man, tall with a beard and longer hair, usually seen wearing a black cape and a top hat, which makes one think of a stage magician. Many claim to smell the aroma of a good cigar when he is around. He is said to appear in the doorways or as a shadow in some of the rooms in the southeast corner of the fourth floor.

The second ghost is said to be the most famous, that of a female in her early thirties named Julia Lowell. It is said she was a prostitute and that she had used the rooms here for her clients. Allegedly, she fell in love with one of her clients, and when she told him, he wanted nothing to do with her. She is said to have committed suicide at the hotel. People claim to have the most experiences with her on the west side of the building on the second and third floors.

There have been men that reported hearing a female voice whispering in their ears. She's been seen dancing in a provocative manner at the foot of the bed, and some say she enjoys playing with men's feet. It can only make you guess what her particular tricks were in her said profession.

The third ghost is one that is never seen, just heard, and that is one of a small boy, around eight or nine years old. Some think he may have had a relative who worked at the hotel. He is thought to be the most mischievous of the ghosts there. Guests on the west side, and on the second and third floors have had reports of objects in their rooms moved from one table to the next, and others say that they hear his footsteps or his laughing.

Regardless, we are sure you will have quite an adventure while staying at the Copper Queen Hotel.

THE COPPER QUEEN HOTEL
11 Howell Avenue, Bisbee, AZ 85603
Phone: (520) 432-2216 Website: http://copperqueen.com/

ARKANSAS

WHERE TO VISIT

PEEL MANSION & HISTORIC GARDENS

The Peel Mansion and Historic Gardens was built in 1875 by Colonel Samuel West Peel. It was erected in the Italianate Villa Style. The interior of the house has been furnished with authentic antiquities and artifacts of the era, which have been loaned by the Historic Arkansas Museum and the Old State House. The site is also an outdoor museum of historic roses, perennials, and native plants. Careful research has resulted in an extensive inventory of nineteenth century plantings.

The museum is said to be haunted by the former owner. There have been reports of light, possibly poltergeists, and corner-of-the-eye apparitions at the museum.

THE PEEL MANSION AND HISTORIC GARDENS
400 South Walton Boulevard, Bentonville, AR 72712
Phone: (479) 273-9664 Website: www.peelmansion.org/

The museum has yearly ghost walks, which can be an exciting way to spend the evening.

Crescent Hotel and Spa. *Photograph courtesy Library of Congress circa 1886*

CRESCENT HOTEL & SPA

This famous Arkansas landmark claims to be America's Most Haunted Hotel, and they have nightly ghost tours, if you are brave enough for the experience.

There are many famous ghosts that reside here, including Michael, an Irish stonemason who fell to his death during the hotels construction, Morris the cat, and mysterious patients from the days when it was a hospital.

The hotel has been featured on Syfy's popular show *Ghost Hunters*, as well as A & E's *Haunted Road Trips*, NBC's *Today Show*, *USA Today*, and Bio Network's *My Ghost Story*.

CRESCENT HOTEL AND SPA
75 Prospect Avenue, Eureka Springs AR 72632
Phone: (877) 342-9766 Website: http://www.crescent-hotel.com/

The nightly tours will share the legendary hauntings of the hotel and there are ongoing investigations. The hotel offers ghost packages, which allow guests to stay the night and for breakfast, as well as taking part in the tour. They also throw in a few mementoes to remember your trip.

CALIFORNIA

★ ★ ★ WHERE TO VISIT ★ ★ ★

COLMA, THE CITY OF THE DEAD

A fan of my writing and lectures told me about a very eerie city just south of San Francisco: Colma, known as "The City of the Dead" or "City of the Souls." Colma is unlike any other in the world, where there is a population of almost 2,000—and another two million underground. Bizarre as it may seem, it has specialized sections, such as a Jewish cemetery, a Chinese cemetery, and a pet cemetery, and it is known that this town has more dead people than living.

Deceased residents of San Francisco were relocated during the turn of the century, as politicians began a campaign to move graveyards out of the city by promoting information that cemeteries spread disease. The real reason for moving them was that they wanted to free up valuable property. California State Law was passed in the late 1800s, State Penal Code 297, an ordinance that said that burials were no longer allowed and, in 1914, eviction notices were sent for all cemeteries to remove their dead and their monuments.

Colma now holds the record of having the most cemeteries in one city, in total, seventeen!

Some famous names can be found in Colma, such as Joe DiMaggio, Wyatt Earp, and many other notable individuals from history, making it a great place for a variety of types of travelers, no matter what interests you happen to have. Among the car dealerships, shopping centers, and local Home Depot, the people who walk above it take pride in the fact they live there, and ironically have the motto: "It's Great to be Alive in Colma!"

COLMA TOWN HALL
1198 El Camino Real, Colma, CA 94014
Phone: (650) 997- 8300 Website: http://www.colma.ca.gov/

Colma, City of the Dead. *Photograph courtesy City of Colma*

Colma, City of the Dead. *Photograph courtesy City of Colma*

Colma, City of the Dead, Cypress Lawn Funeral Home. *Photograph courtesy City of Colma*

Colma, City of the Dead. *Photograph courtesy City of Colma*

LOVED TO DEATH

Established in 2008, Loved to Death is a store that carries taxidermy items, memento mori jewelry (celebrating death), and curiosities, as well as Victorian antiques and art! This interesting little shop has also shown on Discovery's *Oddities* and is the winner of awards, such as the Best of Bay Guardian 2010, and Best Place to Buy Taxidermy You Can Wear. Loved to Death's designs have been worn by people like Francis Bean Cobain, Kat Von D, and Courtney Love. The company has been featured in *Gothic Beauty Magazine, New York Times, LA Weekly, Alt Noir, Rue Morgue,* and *Skin Deep* (a tattoo magazine). This interesting little shop has also been shown on Discovery's *Oddities San Francisco*. Discovery says:

Audra is extremely selective about the items she sells in the shop, only putting the most unique and authentic pieces on her shelves. She began her career working in a natural history store and began her own personal collection from there...Wednesday Mourning is a part-time Goth model, picker, and salesperson whose long-standing obsession with obscurities made her a perfect fit at Loved to Death. As the resident "brainiac," she enjoys researching the origins of bizarre items and often goes into long historical and scientific explanations when explaining them to customers.

Inside the shop you will find The Articulated Gallery, a collection of creepy, but beautiful, art that reminds me of Ripley's Believe it or Not and side-show carny days. If you happen to be in San Francisco, be sure and stop in!

Loved to Death. Wednesday Mourning with customer. *Photograph courtesy Discovery Science Channel*

Audra, owner of Loved to Death. *Photograph courtesy Discovery Science Channel*

LOVED TO DEATH

1681 Haight Street, San Francisco, CA 94117

Phone: (415) 551-1036, Email: info@lovedtodeath.net Websites: www.lovedtodeath.net and www.articulatedgallery.com

This macabre gift shop, located in San Francisco, is open from 11:30 a.m. to 7 p.m. on weekdays, and noon to 7 p.m. on Sundays.

Loved to Death. *Photograph courtesy Discovery Science Channel.*

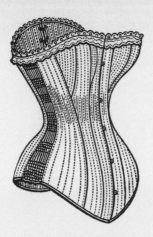

EXOTIC WORLD MUSEUM

The Exotic World Museum or the Burlesque Hall of Fame can be found in Helendale, California. Exotic World originated as the private collection of retired exotic dancer Jennie Lee, now operated by Dixie Evans, a former dancer known as the "Marilyn Monroe of Burlesque." This museum is dedicated to the preservation of the golden age of burlesque when exotic dancing included extravagant costumes and playful choreography. It contains a wealth of striptease and exotic dance memorabilia, including posters, photos, and costumes, including G-strings of famous performers such as Blaze Starr and Chesty "Double Agent 73" Morgan. It even has urns containing the ashes of famous late burlesque stars, and items include ivory fans used by Sally Rand, gloves and a black velvet shoulder cape worn by Gypsy Rose Lee, and the heart-shaped couch owned by Jayne Mansfield. The guide demonstrates moves, lets you in on trade secrets, and tells you anecdotes about the performers honored in the collection. A trip during April will give you a chance to catch the annual Miss Exotic World pageant.

THE BURLESQUE HALL OF FAME
520 E Fremont Street, PO Box #580, Las Vegas, NV 89125
Phone: (888) 661-6465 Website: www.burlesquehall.com

You might like to visit the Exotic Museum due to its bizarreness and place in history.

MUSEUM OF DEATH

Originally located in San Diego's first mortuary, in a building that was once owned by Wyatt Earp, The World Famous Museum of Death was founded in San Diego on June 1, 1995. The museum's founders, James Healy and Cathee Shultz, also house the world's largest collection of serial murderer Artwork, and includes among its treasures photos of the Charles Manson crime scenes, the guillotined severed head of the Blue Beard of Paris, original crime scene and morgue shots from the Black Dhalia murder case, replicas of execution devices, and mortician and autopsy tools.

MUSEUM OF DEATH
6031 Hollywood Boulevard
Hollywood, CA 90028
Phone: 1(323) 466-8011
http://www.museumofdeath.net/

The Museum of Death is a self guided tour and there is no age limit. Hours: Sunday to Friday 11 a.m. to 8 p.m., Saturday 11 a.m. to 10 p.m., $15 admission, with free parking.

FEATURED CALIFORNIA LOCATION!
ALCATRAZ

Alcatraz Island. *Photograph courtesy National Park Services*

This most well known prison, rumored to be filled with restless spirits, is commonly referred to as "The Rock." Alcatraz Island, just off of San Francisco's coastline, received its name in 1775 when the Spanish explorers charted San Francisco bay. In 1847, Alcatraz was taken over by the United States military. The Rock's first prisoners were made up of military convicts. In 1861, Alcatraz started to receive Confederate prisoners; when the war ended, the fort was deemed obsolete and was no longer needed. The prison continued to be used though, and soon, more buildings and cell houses were added. During the 1920s, Alcatraz gradually fell into disuse, until social upheaval and the rampant crime of the 1920s and 1930s, when lead Attorney General Homer Cummings supported J. Edgar Hoover and the FBI in creating a new, escape-proof prison. The attorney general asked James A. Johnston of San Francisco to take over as warden of the new prison, and Johnston implemented a strict set of rules and regulations for the facility. Gun towers were erected at various points around the island and the cellblocks were equipped with catwalks, electric locks, metal detectors, a well-stocked arsenal, barbed wire fencing, and even tear gas containers that were fitted into the ceilings.

Wardens from prisons all over the country were polled and were permitted to send their most incorrigible inmates to the Rock. These included inmates with behavioral problems, those with a history of escape attempts, and even high-profile inmates who were receiving privileges because of their status, such as Al Capone, George "Machine Gun" Kelly, Robert "Birdman of Alcatraz" Stroud, and a member of Bonnie and Clyde's gang.

Alcatraz tourism still thrives here. *Photograph courtesy National Park Services*

Alcatraz was a place of penitence, just as the Quakers who had devised the American prison system had planned for all prisons to be. The guards numbered the inmates one to three, which was high, as most prisons were at least one guard to every twelve inmates. The Hole, as it was known, was located on the bottom tier of cells and was considered to be a severe punishment. Mattresses were taken away and prisoners were sustained by meals of bread and water, supplemented by a solid meal every third day. Closed off from all natural light, it was lit by a low-wattage bulb suspended from the ceiling. Inmates could spend up to nineteen days there, completely silent and isolated from everyone, save for psychological and physical torture from the guards.

Kevin Bacon starred in a film called *Murder in the First* years ago as a prisoner in Alcatraz who left a chilling and deep impact on me to this day. It was based on the true occurrences at the prison. The reality was that the screams from the men being beaten in one of the four cells located on the bottom tier of D Block echoed throughout the block as though being amplified through a megaphone. When men emerged from the darkness and isolation, they would be totally senseless and would

Alcatraz cellblock.
Photograph courtesy
National Park Services

end up in the prison's hospital ward, insane. Others came out with pneumonia and arthritis after spending days to weeks on the cold cement floor with no clothing, and many died there. Prisoners who had the misfortune of being placed in the dungeons were not only locked in, but stripped of their clothing and their dignity, as guards chained them to the wall in a standing position for twelve hours. The only toilet they had was a bucket, which was emptied once each week.

The first years of Alcatraz were known as "the silent years," and during this period, the rules stated that no prisoners were allowed to speak to one another, sing, or whistle. Talking was forbidden in the cells, in the mess hall and even in the showers. The inmates were allowed to talk for three minutes during the morning and afternoon recreation yard periods and for two hours on weekends. Prisoners were not allowed newspapers or magazines that would inform them of current events, but could read from the library.

During the twenty-nine years that Alcatraz was in operation, after riots and countless suicides, there were over fourteen escape attempts in which thirty-four different men risked their lives to escape. (Three made it.) Budget cuts had recently forced security measures at the prison to become more lax. On top of that, the exorbitant cost of running the place continued to increase and over $5 million was going to be needed for renovations. U.S. Attorney General Robert Kennedy declared the prison was no longer necessary. In 1972, Alcatraz became part of the National Park Service. It was opened to the public in the fall of 1973 is now one of the most popular of America's park sites.

Visitors to Alcatraz follow the same path as did the former inmates on their way to what was often their final destination. Many night watchmen who have patrolled the dark cellblocks claim to have heard sounds of what seem to be people running, coming from the upper tiers of the main halls, yet on investigating, they see nothing.

Over the years, many tour guides add to the stories by telling of strange feelings they get at locations like "Hole" cells, such as in the case of cell number 14D. One of the guides claim it is always cold and there is a feeling of sudden intensity that comes from spending more than a few minutes in the area. Former guards mention creepy incidents as far back as the mid 1940s. An inmate was locked in the cell for some forgotten infraction. Rumor has it that the inmate began screaming within seconds of being placed in the cell, claiming there was creature with red glowing eyes there with him. The guards paid no attention and took no pity on the convict, whose screaming continued on into the night...until, at last, there was silence. In the morning, guards entering the cell found the convict dead. A terrified expression was etched on his face, and marks from someone's hands around his throat could be seen. An autopsy revealed that the strangulation could not have been self-inflicted. It is a widespread belief that the inmate was choked by one of the guards, but no one ever admitted it.

Over the passing decades, visitors such as ghost hunters, authors, and many tourists have visited the island and describe weird things that happen there that they cannot explain. Even the park workers, who say they do not believe in ghosts, cannot explain the sounds heard from parts of the facility.

According to a worker who was walking near the shower room, he says he heard the sound of a banjo coming from the room. Al Capone often hid in the shower room to practice playing his banjo, as he feared for his life in the public areas. Capone received permission to remain inside and play. To this day, tour guides walking the empty corridors of the prison claim to hear spectral tunes echoing through the darkness.

ALCATRAZ
Golden Gate National Recreation Area
Fort Mason, B201, San Francisco, CA 94123
Phone: (415) 561-4900 Website: http://www.nps.gov/alca/index.htm

THE
USS HORNET

The USS *Hornet* is said to be one of the most haunted ships in existence. Brought out for combat in 1943, this ship earned a number of decorations by the United States Navy.

Over 300 people lost their lives onboard the mighty vessel, many of which were suicides. The United States Navy has confirmed more suicides occurred on this vessel than any other ship in the naval fleet.

Many have witnessed doors that have strangely opened and closed with no one around. Also, tourists and workers alike claim to have seen personnel dressed in old Navy clothing, suddenly disappearing at night.

USS HORNET
**707 W. Hornet Avenue,
Pier 3, Alameda Point
Alameda, CA 94502
Phone: (510) 521-8448
Website: http://www.uss-hornet.org/**

THE
QUEEN MARY

The Queen Mary is an ocean liner that sailed the North Atlantic Ocean from 1936 to 1967 and is listed on the National Register of Historic Places. Permanently anchored in Long Beach, California, it is both a museum ship and hotel. Long rumored to be a ghost haunt, many areas are reported as having odd occurrences, such as visitors catching the sounds of little children crying in the nursery room and the sound of splashing noises in the drained swimming pool.

THE QUEEN MARY
**Queens Highway
Long Beach, CA 90802
Phone: (877) 342-0742 #1126
Website: http://www.queenmary.com**

Parking is $15/night (self) and $19/night (valet), and no-show reservations will be charged a one-night stay. Check-in is at 4 p.m. with a check-out at 12 p.m. Credit card and ID are required at check-in, and you must be 21 years or older to book rooms aboard.

CHINA FLAT MUSEUM
BIGFOOT COLLECTION

Located at Willow Creek, a small community nestled in the mountainous northwest corner of California, the China Flat Museum on the Hoopa Valley Indian Reservation opened on May 6, 2000. A fascinating museum, you will find items relating to the creature known as Bigfoot. At the opening, keynote speaker and investigator John Green spoke on the legends of Bigfoot.

This location is where Bigfoot sightings were first reported in 1958. Here stands the museum, with its enormous redwood sculpture of Bigfoot, twenty-five feet in height in the parking lot. The museum itself has many items on display as their evidence, including a variety of footprint casts. The Patterson track cast can be seen and is made from one of the footprints left at the 1967 Patterson Gimlin film site in Bluff Creek, California. You will find an assortment of Bigfoot collectables and a growing archive of information, making it one of the largest archives on Bigfoot in the world.

BIGFOOT MUSEUM
5497 Highway 9, Felton, CA 95018
Phone: (530) 629-2653 Website: www.bigfootmuseum.com

Mid-April through the end of October, open Wednesday to Sunday 10 a.m. to 4 p.m.
Free admission, donations accepted. The rest of the year, open by appointment.

Winchester House.
Photograph courtesy Winchester Mystery House

THE
WINCHESTER HOUSE

The infamous Winchester House is one of two homes in California sanctioned by the U.S. Commerce Department as being haunted (the other is the Whaley House, also in this book) The Winchester House is perhaps the most bizarre haunted home in the U.S. It was designed by Sarah Winchester, widow of William Winchester, founder of Winchester rifles. Sarah believed she was cursed by the spirits of those whose deaths were a result of rifles, and the only way to avoid being plagued by them was to build a massive 160-room mansion.

Sarah was deeply affected by the deaths of her daughter, Annie, in 1866, and her husband, William, in 1881. After consulting a medium, who instructed her to build a house to ward off evil spirits, Sarah began the construction of the Winchester House, in 1884, and continued for thirty-eight years, until she died in 1922. During the construction, Sarah held nightly séances to communicate with her dead husband for his opinion on what the house should look like.

When visitors come to see the house, they are greeted by a maze of twisting and turning hallways, multiple dead-ends, secret panels, a floor with a window built into it, staircases leading to nowhere, all with the intention to ward off and confuse ghosts. The house is decorated with a spider web motif—which Sarah believed had some spiritual meaning—and everything from the hooks on the walls to candle holders has been arranged around the number 13. Take a public flashlight tour on Halloween to see it for yourself!

The people behind the movie *The Woman in Black* by Hammer Films Company used the location for their 2012 release of the film.

THE WINCHESTER HOUSE
525 South Winchester Boulevard, San Jose, CA 95128
Phone: (408) 247-2101 Website: http://www.winchestermysteryhouse.com

The Winchester House is located on Winchester Boulevard, between Stevens Creek Boulevard and Interstate 280, south of San Francisco.

Winchester House. *Photograph courtesy Winchester Mystery House*

Winchester House. *Photograph courtesy Winchester Mystery House*

Winchester House. *Photograph courtesy Winchester Mystery House*

HOLLYWOOD FOREVER CEMETERY

This cemetery is the final resting place for the greats of Hollywood's Golden Age. Many say they have had ghost sightings, including those such as actor Rudolph Valentino, who was seen near his crypt. Cold spots have also been felt all over the cemetery. Among those entombed at Hollywood Forever are famous people from the entertainment industry and historic eras of Los Angeles, as well as their relatives. Some of the tombs are quite lavish.

Founded in 1899 on 100 acres as Hollywood Memorial Park Cemetery, in the year 1998, it was renamed Hollywood Forever, and restored. Burials still take place at this lovely cemetery. There is a documentary about the place called *The Young and the Dead,* by director Robert Pulcini that can be found on Amazon.com for purchase. Pick up a map of Hollywood stars' graves at the flower shop at the entrance.

HOLLYWOOD FOREVER CEMETERY
6000 Santa Monica Boulevard, Los Angeles, CA 90038
Phone: (323) 203-0056 Website: hollywoodforever.com

Hollywood Forever Cemetery, in the Hollywood district of the City of Los Angeles, is next to Paramount Studios. During the summer, movies are screened at the cemetery.

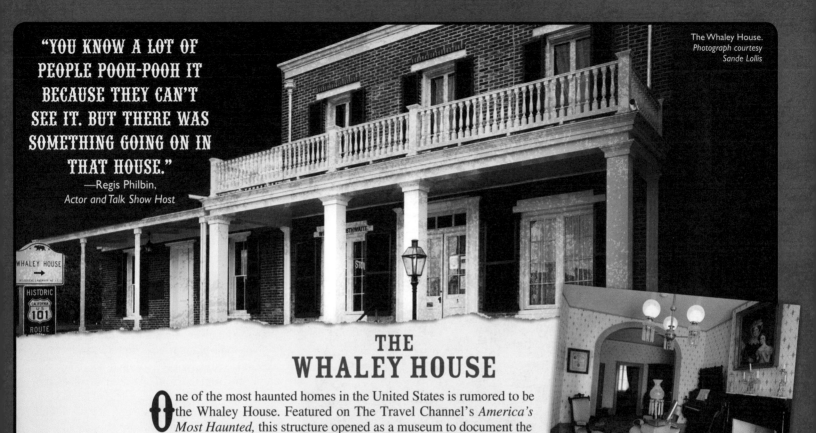

> "YOU KNOW A LOT OF PEOPLE POOH-POOH IT BECAUSE THEY CAN'T SEE IT. BUT THERE WAS SOMETHING GOING ON IN THAT HOUSE."
> —Regis Philbin,
> *Actor and Talk Show Host*

The Whaley House.
*Photograph courtesy
Sande Lollis*

THE WHALEY HOUSE

One of the most haunted homes in the United States is rumored to be the Whaley House. Featured on The Travel Channel's *America's Most Haunted,* this structure opened as a museum to document the history of the building and the paranormal activity that has been said to occur there, most notably spirits such as James "Yankee Jim" Santiago Robinson, who was hanged on a gallows there.

Thomas Whaley, present during the hanging, purchased the property, and then built the house for his family to move into.

Many who have visited claim that the spirit of Thomas Whaley is there, as well as his wife, Anna, and various others, including a man in the parlor area. Many children say they have seen Mr. Whaley. Regis Philbin, the television personality, claimed that he observed the spirit of Anna Whaley on his wall while in his room during his stay in 1964. Regis claimed that he was shaken with excitement and turned on a flashlight to see it better. When he did this, what he'd seen on the wall was completely gone. Other guests and employees of the house say they also have encountered the kindred spirits of Thomas and Anna Whaley.

The Whaley House.
*Photograph courtesy
Sande Lollis*

THE WHALEY HOUSE
2476 San Diego Avenue Old Town, San Diego, CA 92110
Phone: (619) 297-7511 Email: soho-1@sohosandiego.org Website: whaleyhouse.org

Tours are self guided and the hours are seasonal. Admission for daytime tours is $6, evening tours $10. Private tours after 10 p.m. are $75 per person (minimum 2 people) for 1 hour. $50 for each additional hour, limited to 3 hours total; reservations are required.

Preston Castle. *Photograph courtesy Library of Congress*

PRESTON CASTLE

Originally, in 1890, a rehabilitative facility for juveniles who broke the laws, "Preston School of Industry," located in Ione, California, began to accept wayward children into holding cells, in 1894, until it closed in 1960. As time progressed, the abandoned place quickly began deteriorating until a society called Preston Castle Foundation set about restoring the structure shortly after they purchased it. The property was first called Preston School and later renamed, when the property changed hands, as Preston Castle

Not long after, it was rumored to have at least three ghosts, one of which was a female employee from the original school facility from the 1950s. She had been repeatedly kicked over and over again by an inmate until she died. The living quarters of the staff are supposed to be haunted as well. Additionally, there is a cemetery on the grounds for inmates who died at the Preston Castle, totaling twenty-three graves. Many have claimed to have seen spirits there late at night, describing cold spots and feelings of intense fear.

Overnight accommodations are available.

PRESTON CASTLE
Preston Way, Ione, CA 95640
Phone: (408) 207-3612
Email: prestontours@yahoo.com
Website:
www.ghost-trackers.org/castletours.htm

WHERE TO STAY

BIGFOOT CAMPGROUND

After your trek through the Bigfoot Museum, finish your stay at the Bigfoot Campground, a family resort and campground located next to the Bigfoot Scenic Byway. The campground offers a small general store, private cabins with kitchens and bathrooms, as well as spots for RVs and tents.

BIGFOOT CAMPGROUND
Bigfoot Scenic Byway/
Northern California's Trinity River
P.O. Box 280
Junction City CA 96048
Phone: (800) 422-5219 or (530) 623-60888
Email: bigfootrvcabins@snowcrest.net
Website: http://www.bigfootrvcabins.com/

BIGFOOT MOTEL

The Bigfoot Motel is part of the Six Rivers National Forest, a beautiful wilderness retreat on Willow Creek, and is the favorite place to stay for Bigfoot investigators and curious vacationers, who often make the spot their starting point. Not only is it modernized, unlike the campgrounds that use the same name, it boasts restaurants and shops within walking distance.

BIG FOOT MOTEL
39039 California 299
Willow Creek, CA 95573
Phone: (530) 629-2142
Website: www.bigfootmotel.com

Not far away you can visit The Willow Creek—
China Flat Museum, which has a large display for Bigfoot.

COLORADO

WHERE TO VISIT

★ ★ ★   ★ ★ ★

ST. ELMO GHOST TOWN

There is no longer an actual town nestled at the base of Chalk Creek in St. Elmo, Colorado. However, it is rumored that many of the ghosts of previous residents still linger there.

Many different visitors report multiple "cold" spots that may indicate a hot spot for ghosts, and say that there is a ghost that looks at them from a window on the second floor. Her name is believed to be Annabelle.

This fascinating ghost town is privately owned, but the owners allow visitors. There are also shopping opportunities at a store selling general merchandise during your visit.

ST. ELMO GHOST TOWN
Chaffee Road, 2WD, St. Elmo, CO 81236
Website: www.ghosttowns.com/states/co/saintelmo.html]

The town is normally open from May to October annually.

The Stanley Hotel.
Photograph courtesy Library of Congress

★ ★ ★ WHERE TO STAY ★ ★ ★

THE STANLEY HOTEL

The stately Stanley Hotel, overlooking the Rocky Mountains in Estes Park, Colorado, is where author Stephen King received his inspiration for his horror novel, *The Shining*. Actor Jack Nicholson portrayed Jack Torrance in the first rendition of the movie of that same name, the hotel caretaker who goes mad during a long winter at an isolated mountain resort.

In honor of the anniversary of *The Shining*, the Stanley offered a Halloween weekend with many activities. The main event was the Shining Ball, complete with a costume contest.

Staff who work in the kitchen, next to the ballroom, after hours say they have heard a party in empty rooms, and guests claim that they have seen ghosts in their rooms. Sometimes, people claim to hear the piano playing when no one is there from the ballroom.

This is the place to learn more about Stephen King's connection to the hotel, including room 217 where he was inspired to write his novel. Also visit the hotel's most haunted spots, such as the underground tunnel.

THE STANLEY HOTEL
333 Wonderview Avenue, Estes Park, CO 80517
Phone: (800) 976-1377 Email: info@stanleyhotel.com Website: www.stanleyhotel.com/

To book your tour, call (970) 577-4111 to speak to a tour guide. Ghost tours are open to the public. Stanley Hotel Museum and Archive Room reservations are required ahead of time. Order a "Redrum" cocktail, and if you arrive early on Friday, enjoy a private viewing of *The Shining (1980)*. Redrum Punch, a pineapple-flavored drink spiked with several types of rum, is always available.

CONNECTICUT

★★★ WHERE TO VISIT ★★★

WITCH'S DUNGEON
CLASSIC MOVIE MUSEUM

In Bristol, Connecticut, see the figure of actor Bela Lugosi, "Count Dracula," at The Witch's Dungeon Classic Movie Museum. Open weekends during October since 1966, Victoria Price and Sara Karloff, daughters of the famous actors Vincent Price and Boris Karloff, have visited to see the wax displays of their parent depicted in scenes from past films.

The owner, Mr. Hull, whose father helped him build this amazing place tells me that:

it is a non-profit attraction to tribute the makeup artists and actors, such as Boris Karloff, Bela Lugosi, Lon Chaney, Vincent Price, and others, who gave us the classic chillers of the movies. This wax museum-style exhibit is considered the longest running Halloween attraction in the country.

Each figure is accurate to the film, the heads are based on life casts of the actors, some with original costumes or props, each in a scene based on the film. Special audio tracks by Vincent Price, Mark Hamill, and June Foray guide you through the tour. Occasionally the families of Karloff, Lugosi, and Chaney may be present to greet visitors.

WITCH'S DUNGEON CLASSIC MOVIE MUSEUM
90 Battle Street, Bristol, CT 0510, Phone: (860) 583-8306
Website: www.preservehollywood.com Email: witchsdungeon@sbcglobal.net

Hours are from 7 p.m. to 10 p.m. weekend evenings, during October, for a $2.00 donation.

Witches Dungeon, Phantom of the Opera.
Photograph courtesy Cordtlant Hull

Witches Dungeon, Bela Lugosi.
Photograph courtesy Cordtlant Hull.

Witches Dungeon, Boris Karloff.
Photograph courtesy Cordtlant Hull.

Witches Dungeon, Dr. Phibes.
Photograph courtesy Cordtlant Hull.

★ ★ ★ WHERE TO STAY ★ ★ ★

THE
BENTON
HOMESTEAD

This 1720 New England-style home is rumored to be a haunted house. Visitors hear crying, said to be Jemima Barrows, fiancé of a returning solider from the Revolutionary War, and people also hear sounds of a person walking when no one is there. Visitors claim to hear distant voices and whispers.

DANIEL BENTON HOMESTEAD
160 Metcalf Road, Tolland, CT 06084
Phone: (860) 974-1875
Website: http://pages.cthome.net/
tollandhistorical/Benton.htm

THE
LIGHTHOUSE INN

The Lighthouse Inn, said to be one of the most haunted places in Connecticut, is located in New London. It was constructed in the year 1902 and is a site of intrigue among paranormal investigators.

When the inn opened in 1927, it was so large and luxurious that it became quite popular among socially-elite individuals, such as Bette Davis and Joan Crawford, who were said to be visitors at the exquisitely designed mansion.

Back in the year of 1930, a couple was to be married at the mansion. As the bride walked down the staircase, she accidently fell to her death. Employees and locals say that the bride has never left, claiming to have seen her spirit in a beautiful wedding gown moving throughout the building. There are those who have also said that they have heard the spirit laughing and even smell her perfume.

THE LIGHTHOUSE INN
6 Guthrie Place (Lower Boulevard and Guthrie Place)
New London, CT 06320 Phone: (888) 443-8411
Website: www.ctafterdark.com/hotelinfo/77037.htm

Pea Patch Island, Fort Delaware.
Photograph courtesy Library of Congress

DELAWARE

★ ★ ★ WHERE TO VISIT ★ ★ ★

PEA PATCH ISLAND, FORT DELAWARE

Fort Delaware is located along the Delaware Bay in Delaware City. Finished two years before the start of the Civil War, the imposing structure covers six acres with high walls around the building. While not originally built as a prison camp, it actually became one during the war, as prisoners started to arrive in 1862, with a large number arriving after the Battle of Gettysburg in 1863. By the end of the war, thousands of men had been prisoners.

Life in the camp was tough. Prisoners would live in wooden huts that were in bad shape: during the rain, the prisoners would not be able to stay dry, and during the winter months, they wouldn't be able to stay warm. It had a high mortality rate with reports of over 2,500 prisoners dying there.

With so much anguish happening at the fort, there is obviously going to be much reported paranormal activity. In the basement, people claim to hear chains rattling, voices, moans, and there have even been claims of full-body apparitions of Confederate soldiers. There have been many pictures taken at the fort with mists and orbs, as well as some that allegedly have the presence of a soldier in them.

Some claim to have seen the apparition of a woman and child in one of the buildings, as well as the laughing of children being heard. There are reports of people being touched around the fort. In fact, there are so many reports that the park now offers candlelight ghost tours during the summer.

I would encourage any of you to experience the ghost tour to hear all of the best stories that can be told by those who are closest to the fort. You never know; you may have an experience to share with others, too, by the end of the night.

FORT DELAWARE
45 Clinton Street, Delaware City, DE 19706
Phone: (302) 834-7941 Website: www.destateparks.com/park/fort-delaware

FLORIDA

★ ★ ★ WHERE TO VISIT ★ ★ ★

SAINT AUGUSTINE

When many people think of haunted American cities, New Orleans probably comes straight to mind, but right up there on the list should be America's oldest city, Saint Augustine, Florida. Saint Augustine's long and sordid history is also a haunted history. People flock here to witness or experience the paranormal by staying at a haunted bed and breakfast, by visiting many of the sites reputed to be haunted, or by taking a late night ghost tour. You can even call (904) 377-3800 to reserve a hearse tour (www.hearseghosttours.com) to see the sights. An eerie car will take you on an hour and a half ride through cemeteries and historic sights of town while you listen to grisly tales!

Saint Augustine, Ghosts and Gravestones Historic Tours. *Photograph courtesy Haunted Tours Ghost Diggers*

CASTILLO DE SAN MARCOS

At the Castillo de San Marcos, the first stone was laid in 1672, and construction ended in 1695, so being as old as it is, and considering all that has happened during its time, it is no surprise that this place is reported to be haunted.

It is said that, in one of the watchtowers, a light shines out on nights when it storms, but there is no power that goes to that light. People have also claimed to have seen Spanish soldiers dressed in the garb of their era. Additionally, there are those who say they have been touched or have felt strange feelings while in the dungeon of the fort.

Visiting this place actually takes you back to another time, and while you are in some of the rooms, such as the prison or the housing quarters, you have a sense that you are not alone. The best time to visit is near to closing, especially during the fall. During this time, you have a feeling that you are being watched, and that events are occurring all around you, even though you can only see something from the corner of your eye.

I personally have always enjoyed my visits to the fort, much like all of my visits to Saint Augustine in general. You will never be disappointed that you made the visit.

CASTILLO DE SAN MARCOS
1 S. Castillo Drive, St. Augustine, FL 32084
Phone: (904) 829-6506 Website: http://www.nps.gov/casa/index.htm

Hours are Monday to Sunday: 8:45 a.m. to 5:15 p.m.

Saint Augustine lighthouse.
*Photograph courtesy Haunted
Tours Ghost Diggers*

SAINT AUGUSTINE LIGHTHOUSE

Of all of the places in Florida, one that is seen to be the most haunted is the Saint Augustine Lighthouse. It has been featured on television shows, such as *Ghost Hunters,* and that program even provided some strong evidence of the hauntings taking place there.

The tower, as it exists today, was built from 1871 through 1874. Fire was set to the structure in 1971, but a group came in, refurbished the lighthouse and surrounding structures, and turned it into a museum.

People visiting the lighthouse are said to have experienced many hauntings. One is that of several children wandering the grounds. One child is known to have died on the grounds, and it is thought that this child still haunts the establishment.

With many places reputed to be haunted, you don't always get the sense of haunting during the daylight hours, but this is not the case at the lighthouse. Here, you always get the sense that there is someone around you.

I have had the pleasure of visiting here on more than one occasion, and have always been pleased. The staff is friendly, the displays are remarkable, and the sense that you are not alone is priceless.

SAINT AUGUSTINE LIGHTHOUSE
82 Lighthouse Avenue, Saint Augustine, FL 32080
Phone: (904) 829-0745
Website: http://www.staugustinelighthouse.com/

It is recommended that you allow at least one hour to tour the site and climb the tower. The last ticket to climb the tower is sold at 5:45 p.m. The site closes at 6 p.m. During the summer and many holidays the Lighthouse is open until 7 p.m., with the last ticket being sold at 6:45 p.m. Closed Thanksgiving Day, Christmas Eve, and Christmas Day. Tickets: $9.50, seniors 60+ $7.50, and children 12 and under $7.50.

RIPLEY'S
BELIEVE IT OR NOT MUSEUM

I love going to Ripley's Museums across the country. When I come across a city that has one, I have to visit. There are museums in the Wisconsin Dells, Hollywood, Niagara Falls, Gatlinburg, Key West and Orlando, and other places. My favorite of all is the museum in Saint Augustine, an amazing city with a fascinating history.

The museum is located inside Castle Warden, a historic Moorish Revival-style mansion that was built as a winter home for William Warden, a millionaire who spent his winters in the area. It later served as a high-class hotel, before being bought by Ripley's to serve as a museum.

Two women died in a fire while it was still a hotel in 1944. Some believe the women were murdered and the fire was set to cover up the killings.

There is an area of the museum, which, at the current time, houses an optical illusion of a woman in a shower, where you definitely feel that *something* is around you. I am not certain if this is where the fire took place; I have been told that it was, but have no real confirmation. Every time that I visit the museum, I feel something around me when at this exhibit and the close surrounding area. There definitely appears to be a presence on the second floor. I am not alone in saying this: people who have worked at the museum or who have visited have claimed to hear a woman sobbing or other sounds a woman might make coming from the second floor.

RIPLEY'S BELIEVE IT OR NOT MUSEUM
19 San Marco Avenue, St. Augustine, FL 32084
Phone: (904) 824-1606 Email: mock@ripleys.com
Website: http://www.ripleys.com/staugustine/

THE
OLD JAIL

Built in 1891 for prisoners, The Old Jail is a ghost hunters' top travel destination. Today, The Old Jail is open to the public as a museum where visitors can tour the structure, observing where prisoners were kept for over sixty years, gaze on the gallows, and more!

The Old Jail is listed in the *National Directory of Haunted Places,* and the *National Registry of Historic Places.* As the historic tours website says:

Discover the history behind judicial practices in the 19th century and see an array of weapons and artifacts. Adults and children are thoroughly entertained by our costumed actors who portray deputies from the early days and everyone gets a chance to try and escape! The Old Jail is one of just a few prisons of its kind still standing and makes for a great sightseeing and history adventure.

As the conditions at the structure were harsh, and many inmates died of sickness while staying here, it is obvious why the spirits still haunt the establishment.

Theresa Stratford, the Director of Marketing for Bulldog Tours commented, "I would say the most striking aspect of the Old City Jail is just the way it looks very creepy and dark from the outside," and I for one quite agree with her!

THE OLD JAIL
167 San Marco Avenue, St. Augustine, FL 32084
Phone: (904) 829-3800
Website: http://www.historictours.com/staugustine/

Both Images: Saint Augustine Old Jail.
Photograph courtesy Haunted Tours Ghost Diggers

SPOOK HILL
LAKE WALES

While it costs a fee to visit most attractions in Florida, this is a place to visit that won't cost you a thing.

Spook Hill is a gravity hill. When you put your car in neutral, it appears to coast uphill. The locals also have legends to explain it. The sign at the hill states:

Many years ago an Indian village on Lake Wales was plagued by raids of a huge gator. The Chief, a great warrior, killed the gator in a battle that created a small lake. The chief was buried on the north side. Pioneer mail riders first discovered their horses laboring downhill, thus naming it Spook Hill. When the road was paved, cars coasted up hill. Is this the gator seeking revenge, or the chief still trying to protect his land?

If you are looking for something off the beaten path, then Spook Hill is the place for you.

SPOOK HILL
5th Street, Lake Wales, FL 33853

From S.R. 17, turn east onto J.A. Wiltshire to 5th Street.

THE
RIDDLE HOUSE

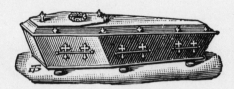

In the early 1900s, the Riddle House was built as a funeral parlor for families who had lost loved ones.

Karl Riddle eventually became the overseer for the cemetery located on the property, and he was provided a home to live in called the "Gatekeeper's Cottage"...until an employee committed suicide there. The Riddle family left and several different businesses attempted to start in the same building, but all of them failed.

Karl Riddle's nephew, John, decided to preserve it as a historical monument for the public. Carpenters and other workers experienced many strange things while renovating it, like tools being moved, broken windows, and many of the workers quit.

If you are around the Palm Beach Fairgrounds, be sure to stop by the Yesteryear Village and go to the Riddle House to explore!

THE RIDDLE HOUSE
Yesteryear Village, Palm Beach Fairgrounds
9067 Southern Boulevard, West Palm Beach, FL 33411
Phone: (561) 795-6400
Website: http://www.southfloridafair.com/

WHERE TO EAT

★ ★ ★　　　　　　　　　　　★ ★ ★

MONSTERS CAFE

I love horror films and feel that there were never a finer set of films than those having the monsters that were depicted in the classic Universal films from the 1930s, 1940s, and 1950s. These films had a sense of both elegance and horror that no one has been able to top since.

If you love the classic cinema monsters such as Dracula, Frankenstein, the Wolf Man, the Mummy, the Invisible Man, and the Creature from the Black Lagoon, then there is no a greater place to enjoy them all at one place than the Monsters Café located at Universal Studios in Orlando, Florida.

There are different areas set up with great memorabilia from the classic horror films that many of us grew up with. I always seem to spend my time dedicated to Frankenstein in the castle area, but the swamp is also great. I have enjoyed dining here with each of my visits to Universal Studios, Orlando. My last visit occurred during their Halloween Nights, a perfect time. The food is counter service with old favorites like rotisserie chicken, brick oven pizza, and salads.

So if you are on your Orlando vacation, you need to spend at least a day at Universal Studios and have a meal here. You will not regret it.

MONSTERS CAFE
6000 Universal Boulevard, Orlando, Florida 32819
Phone: (407) 363-8000 Email: http://www.visitorsatisfaction.com/contactus/
Website: http://www.universalorlando.com/Restaurants/Universal-Studios-Florida/production-central-dining.aspx

WHERE TO STAY

CASABLANCA
INN BED & BREAKFAST

Historic Casablanca Inn Bed and Breakfast, built in 1914, is listed in the National Register of Historic Places. The house has great views of Mantanzas Bay, where you can watch the boats pass by. Besides being a great place to relax and enjoy your trip, it is also a place reported to be haunted.

The story is that during prohibition, a widow who owned the house became entangled people who were involved with bootleggers, and she was intimate with one of them. Since many wanted their spirits, and the financial reward was as big as it was, she helped out her friends and would take a cut of the profits. The widow would go to the top of the building at night, and if government officials, who were trying to break up the bootleggers operations, were in town, she would wave her lantern back and forth to warn her friends. They, in turn, would pass on safely without fear of arrest.

It is said today that many people see a light still coming from the Casablanca Inn, whether it be people staying at other hotels, or boats passing through the city. It appears that the widow's spirit has held on, as she continues to warn her friends on the other side.

CASABLANCA INN BED AND BREAKFAST
24 Avenida Menendez, Saint Augustine, Florida 32084
Phone: (800) 826-2626 Email: innkeeper@casablancainn.com
Website: www.casablancainn.com

The Andersonville Prison.
Photograph courtesy Library of Congress

GEORGIA

AS IN ST. AUGUSTINE, FLORIDA, YOU CAN CALL (912) 695-1578 TO RESERVE A HEARSE TOUR OF SAVANNAH, GEORGIA (WWW.HEARSEGHOSTTOURS.COM) TO SEE LOCAL SIGHTS AS IT PASSES THROUGH CEMETERIES AND HISTORIC PLACES, AND LISTEN TO GRISLY TALES DURING YOUR HOUR AND A HALF RIDE!

★ ★ ★ WHERE TO VISIT ★ ★ ★

THE ANDERSONVILLE PRISON

Each state has a site that it claims is one of the most haunted "Where to Visit." Many times this place would be an old jail, hospital, or home. Georgia is no exception. Their site would be the Andersonville Prison, a national historic site where Union soldiers were once held as prisoners of war.

As the prison once housed soldiers captured in battle, who were brought to this facility and were then further abused, it should come as no surprise that there are many hauntings reported at the facility.

A story goes that there were many individuals given a position of command at the camp who were referred to as "Raiders," and that they were not even Confederates, but just regular prisoners at the facility. These people allegedly would randomly torture individuals there with harsh beatings, also taking their food and clothing, and, at times, would even kill others.

It is reported that in the evening hours, you can hear the echoes of gun fire and experience strong feelings of devastation and fear. Many claim to hear faint whispers, loud cries, and even yelling. There is a theory in the field of paranormal research that many hauntings are residual, that it is like a tape replaying the past over and over again. This appears to be the case at the prison.

Stop by this amazing place and see if you experience what others do.

ANDERSONVILLE NATIONAL HISTORIC SITE
Route 1, Andersonville, GA 31711

THE ANDERSONVILLE PRISON
496 Cemetery Road, Andersonville, GA 31711 Phone: (912) 924-0343
Facebook: facebook.com/AndersonvilleNPS/ Website: http://www.nps.gov/ande/index.htm

The facility is open year round with the exception of Thanksgiving, New Year's Day, and Christmas.

MOON RIVER BREWING COMPANY

In 2003, Savannah was named the most haunted city in America by the American Institute of Paranormal Psychology. The most haunted place in Savannah is said to be the Moon River Brewing Company.

The brewery was featured in the 2005 Halloween Special of the popular Syfy series *Ghost Hunters*, as well as on the Travel Channel's *Ghost Adventures*. The restaurant is happy to share ghost stories with the public, rather than hiding it. Visit their website to read some of the stories.

The restaurant has an excellent menu at reasonable prices, as well as an outstanding beer selection, brewed on the premises.

While in the most haunted city in America, be sure to visit the most haunted restaurant in town.

MOON RIVER BREWING COMPANY
21 W. Bay Street, Savannah, GA 31401
Phone: (912) 447-0943
E-mail: info@moonriverbrewing.com
Website: http://moonriverbrewing.com/

Hours: Sunday to Thursday: 11 a.m. to 11 p.m,
Friday and Saturday: 11 a.m. to midnight

BONAVENTURE CEMETERY

This cemetery was filmed in a movie called *Midnight in the Garden of Good and Evil*, and is considered one of the most haunted cemeteries in Savannah, Georgia. Prior to it becoming a cemetery, it was first a huge plantation owned by Josiah Tattnall, Jr. One night, the immense mansion caught fire. In today's cemetery, many visitors to its grounds claim they can hear voices of people socializing, as if at the plantation's lavish parties. If you are in the area, you might want to check it out for yourself.

BONAVENTURE CEMETERY
330 Bonaventure Road, Savannah, GA 31404
Phone: (912) 651-6843 or (866) 666-DEAD
Website: http://www.bonaventurecemeterytours.com/

Daily Tours: Contact the main office as hours are subject to change.
Office hours 10 a.m. to 10 p.m.

IDAHO

★ ★ ★ WHERE TO VISIT ★ ★ ★

The Idaho State Penitentiary "Old Pen." *Photograph courtesy of Idaho State Archives*

THE IDAHO STATE PENITENTIARY

In 1870, this massive structure was constructed in an effort to control the criminals in and around the area of Boise.

One of the most common of all of the rumors of haunting occur at the chambers of the executioner, and many who tour the facility have to end their tour here because they just cannot continue on. Visitors say they can feel the inmates and old guards. The building is often frequented by ghost hunters all over the country.

THE IDAHO STATE PENITENTIARY
(Also called the Old Penitentiary by the State Historical Society)
(Formal Address) 2445 Old Penitentiary Road, Boise, ID 83712
Phone: (208) 334-2844 Website: http://history.idaho.gov/old-penitentiary-hours-location

If you would like to visit, they are located on Warm Springs east of Boise (per the Historical Society).
Free parking is available. Regular Hours, noon to 5 p.m. Last admission at 4:15 p.m. Closed on New Year's Day,
President's Day, Columbus Day, Veteran's Day, Thanksgiving Day, Christmas Day. Admission Prices:
Adults: $5, Seniors: (60 and older) $4, Child (6-12 years): $3, Children under 6 free.

WHERE TO STAY

THE
BATES MOTEL

Regardless if you have a frightening experience or not, just staying at a place called the Bates Motel should be exciting to anyone. You can tell your friends you stayed at a motel that shares the same name as the one from the famous movie *Psycho*.

The building that houses the motel was originally a barracks for officers at the Farragut Naval Training Station. After World War II, the building was sold and after some amount of time, Randy Bates bought the building and called it the Bates Motel.

The sign in the front has a stylized silhouette of Norman Bates's house from the movie. Sometimes, during Halloween, the motel will create a haunted house or may just have mannequins that wear costumes.

So, while you are in Idaho, be sure to stay at the Bates Motel, and when you arrive, be sure to say that Mother sent you.

THE BATES MOTEL
2018 E. Sherman Avenue, Coeur d'Alene, ID 83814
Phone: (208) 667-1411 Email: thebatesmotel@adelphia.net
Website: www.thebatesmotel.com

ILLINOIS

WHERE TO VISIT

★ ★ ★   ★ ★ ★

RESURRECTION CEMETERY

Chicago is home to some of the most famous ghosts in the country. One of the most famous is that of Resurrection Mary, considered by many to be the Mary in the original hitchhiker ghost story. In Justice, Illinois, travelers report seeing a young blonde girl walking by; they have offered to give her a ride. The girl is said to accept the ride, but soon disappears. The ghost is thought by some to be the spirit of a young Polish girl, named Mary Bregovy, who was killed in an auto accident in 1934.

RESURRECTION CEMETERY
7201 Archer Avenue, Justice, IL 60458
Phone: (708) 458-4770
Website: catholiccemeterieschicago.org

Office Hours: 8:30 a.m. to 4 p.m. Monday to Friday; 9 a.m. to 1 p.m. Saturday

COOK COUNTY JAIL

Little Village is Chicago's largest Mexican-American community in a two-mile stretch of 26th Street. There you will find a jail that opened on April Fool's Day, 1929, but is no longer housing criminals. Over the years, however, the Cook County Jail housed numerous celebrity criminals. Infamous mob boss Al Capone was sent to Cook County Jail on October 24, 1931, on charges of tax evasion and to violating the Volstead Act. John Wayne Gacy was a serial killer who murdered thirty-three boys and men between 1972 and 1978. Also known as the Killer Clown, once the murderer was caught, his trial took place at Cook County Court and he was held at the jail during his trial.

Another famous inmate was Tommy O'Connor, who was arrested, in 1921, for killing a policeman, and was sent to Cook County Jail. Found guilty at his trial, O'Connor was sentenced to hang, but just four days before, he and four other inmates escaped, and were never captured—although people claim to have seen him until the 1930s. There is a tombstone for Tommy O'Connor dated 1951, in Illinois, but no one knows how he died.

COOK COUNTY SHERIFF'S OFFICE
50 W. Washington, Chicago, IL 60602
Phone: (312) 603-6444 Email: sheriff.dart@cookcountyil.gov
Website: http://www.cookcountysheriff.org/doc/doc_main.html

GEORGE STICKNEY HOUSE

THE WITCH'S GRAVE

George Stickney House, located in Bull Valley, Illinois, listed on the *National Register of Historic Places* since 1979, has a unique design due to Stickney's belief in spiritualism. George and his wife wished to communicate with their dead children, and the family conducted séances on the second floor. Nine of the children died tragically. They believed that the spirits in his house required the freedom to roam without getting caught on corners, so the entire home has rounded corners.

Today, the house is the local police department, and it is claimed that police officers report strange sounds, objects moving around, lights turning off, and door knobs turning when no one is around.

The Village of Bull Valley and its police department have admitted to strange occurrences in the old Stickney House. In 2005, Bull Valley Police Chief Norbert Sauers described his knowledge of experiences, possibly paranormal, at the Stickney Mansion. Sauers said that village employees have heard numerous sounds that seem to defy explanation. He described "…hearing footsteps in the second floor ballroom, a room that today is used only as storage for village records," which was used for séances when the Stickney's owned the mansion. The Chief said he has personally "…experienced objects moving around on his desk, lights turning off, door knobs turning and a door opening, seemingly by themselves, and voices from thin air."Another police officer in Bull Valley claims to have come face-to-face with an apparition of Stickney's father-in-law.

THE GEORGE STICKNEY HOUSE
Currently the Bull Valley Police Department
1904 Cherry Valley Road, Woodstock, IL 60098
Phone: (815) 459-4728 Website: stickneyhousefoundation.org/History.html

Also of interest, the nearby Holcombville Cemetery is where the tombs of the Stickney children are located.

The Witch's Grave can be found in the small town of Chesterville, located west of Arcola, in the heart of Illinois Amish country. Just outside of the village, and across an ancient, one-lane bridge is the tiny Chesterville Cemetery, where one can find "the witch's grave." The story locally is that it is the resting place of a young woman who liked to challenge the Amish faith, speaking out against the treatment of women and continually disobeying the elders of the church. She was banished, and soon after, she disappeared. Later, her body was discovered in a farmer's field and placed in the local funeral home. Curious people from all over came to view.

Another local legend says that a woman was practicing witchcraft and put to death. It is said that her spirit continues to haunt the place and that you can see a white outline of her former self there at night.

CHESTERVILLE CEMETERY
378-398 N. County Road 450 E
Arthur, IL 61911

INDIANA

WHERE TO VISIT

WHISPERS ESTATE

Whispers Estate is a Victorian-designed home located in Mitchell, constructed in the year of 1899. It was originally the home of Dr. John Gibbons and his wife, Jessie. This couple simply adored children, especially the 10-year-old girl they adopted named Rachael. One afternoon, Rachael started a devastating fire in the parlor. She suffered from intense burns and died.

Visitors claim they have seen the girl around the Whispers Estate. In 2006, the beautiful Victorian home was purchased by an individual who elected to renovate it into a bed and breakfast. Soon, guests spread the word that they heard whispers while staying there, thus the building was named "Whispers Estates." It no longer operates as a bed and breakfast, but it can be toured.

Many of the reported paranormal experiences here have been documented by the employees, guests, and locals. The estate has been covered on Travel Channel's *Most Terrifying Places*, The SyFy Channel's *SPOOKED TV* episode "Children of the Grave," as well as having been highlighted on the DVD, *Ghost Stories 2: Unmasking the Dead*.

WHISPERS ESTATE
800-898 West Warren Street, Mitchell, Indiana 46282
Phone: (317) 863-0874 or (855) 55-SPOOK (855-557-7665) Website: http://whispersestate.com/

Willard Library.
Photograph courtesy Library of Congress

WILLARD LIBRARY

Willard Library is the oldest public library in Indiana, established in 1885 in Evansville. Listed in the National Register of Historic Places, it is rumored to have a ghost, called the "Grey Lady Ghost."

The Willard Library Ghost has brought thousands of people to the library offering a virtual tour with Greg Hager, the Willard Library Director.

WILLARD LIBRARY
**21 First Avenue
Evansville, IN 47710
Phone: (812) 425-4309
Email: willard@willard.lib.in.us
Website: www.willard.lib.in.us**

Call for tour times as they are subject to change.

WHERE TO STAY

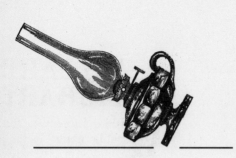

THE HANNAH HOUSE

Many ghost hunters have investigated The Hannah House. It dates back to the time period of the Underground Railroad, when slaves often took refuge in the basement of this home on their journey toward freedom. One evening, a runaway knocked a lantern over and a fire engulfed the basement, and most of the slaves were killed. To remain hidden from prying eyes, the owners of the home buried the slaves on the property so that they would not be found.

Locals say it was once used as a hotel where gangsters took their girlfriends. Visitors claim to have witnessed poltergeist activities, such as windows and doors randomly opening and closing when no one else was there. They've experienced drafts and have reported the smell of death and that of rotting flesh.

If you are interested in spending the night in haunted places and getting a feel for the spiritual side, lodging is available at the beautiful Hannah House!

HANNAH HOUSE
3801 Madison Avenue, Indianapolis, IN 46227
Phone: (317) 787-8486 Website: thehannahmansion.org

Overnight stays are from 9 p.m. until 5 a.m. The cost is $50 per person.
Please see their website for available dates.

THE BARBEE HOTEL & RESTAURANT

Legend has it that the Barbee Hotel on Barbee Lake, outside of Warsaw, Indiana, was a popular spot for Chicago gangsters from the 1920s, including Al Capone.

Many believe that some of the gangsters have remained in the hotel after their deaths. Staff members have supposedly seen an old man in a booth after closing, and when talking to him, they get no response. Believing they are dealing with an unruly customer, they leave to get help to run the patron out. However, when they return, the bar is empty and no one remembers seeing the old man leave.

Another legend is that one of the gangster's girlfriends was killed at the hotel and that she continues to haunt the place.

There are also reports that ghostly faces appear in photographs taken inside the hotel, as well as orbs. It has been a popular place for ghost hunting groups to investigate, due to these alleged hauntings.

I have had the pleasure of dining at the restaurant and can assure you that the food is all top-notch and the atmosphere is very classy. If you are in the area, you must take the time to experience the same atmosphere that the famous gangsters of the past relished.

THE BARBEE HOTEL AND RESTAURANT
3620 N. Barbee Road, Warsaw, IN 46582
Phone: (574) 834-1111 Email: barbeehotel1@aol.com
Website: www. barbeehotel.com

IOWA

WHERE TO VISIT

MOORE HOUSE

The supposedly haunted house of Villisca is located in a remote corner of Iowa that was once a booming town. It was hit with tragedy on June 10, 1912.

The Moore family was highly respected and revered in the city. Josiah Moore and his wife, Sarah, were well known and liked. One day, they left a Children's Day Program event that Sarah had organized in the community to go home.

The next morning, a neighbor to the Moore's, Mary Peckham, noticed that the home was unusually silent, so she went to check on them. Ms. Peckham attempted to get someone to come to the door, and even tried to peer inside the windows, until another family member arrived to unlock the home. They began to search through the home, and found their dead bodies. The family had been murdered by way of an ax to the head.

Visitors to the house claim to hear the sound of children playing and laughing and faint whispers in the home. In 2013, the current owners celebrated its 100th anniversary and local media covered the event the entire week before my call for details!

MOORE HOUSE
508 East 2nd Street, Villisca, IA 50864
Phone: (712) 621-1530 Email: dmlinn@wildblue.net Website: www.villiscaiowa.com/

Daytime tours (seasonal) $10, evening lamp-lit tours are by reservation and are only $25. The price for an individual daytime tour of the house is $10.00 per person 12 and over, children 7-11 are $5, and seniors 65 and over are $5. Overnight stays by reservation only $300 for up to 5 guests, $60 for each additional guest. During the tour season, which runs from March 1st to November 1st, the house is open daily from 1 p.m. to 4 p.m. Tuesday thru Friday, and from 1 p.m. to 4 p.m. on Saturday and Sunday. Closed Mondays. Walk-in tours of the house will be conducted on a first-come, first-serve basis. From November 1st until March 1st, all daytime tours are closed.

WHERE TO STAY

MASON HOUSE INN

Ibelieve that whatever energy comes into a building stays with that building. Think of visiting a house where people are happy. You get a good feeling from the building. Now think about one where people are always fighting or are unhappy. You can sense that from the moment you walk in. Hotels have an even stronger amount of energy within them than other places, as they have a large number of people passing through their halls.

The Mason House in Iowa is reputed to be one of the most haunted places in the state. The current owners are Chuck and Joy Hanson, and they have given interviews sharing the stories of hauntings and their personal experiences with running the establishment.

There are stories of people tugging at the bed when there is no one else in the room. The spirit of a young teenage boy is seen by many of the guests and staff. He apparently likes to knock on doors.

Allegedly there are many people who have strong negative feelings when they come into Room 7. It is reported that a man was murdered in the room.

Other guests experience seeing foggy apparitions. There are many reports of touching coming from someone who is not there.

The Inn has murder mystery weekends where you can play an amateur sleuth in a fun game of "whodunit." If you love a good mystery, you must call and find out when they are having their next event. Lastly, during the Halloween season, they have a Halloween Ghost Dinner.

MASON HOUSE INN
21982 Hawk Drive, Bentonsport, IA 52565
Phone: (319) 592-3133; for reservations: (1-800) 592-3133
Email: Stay@MasonHouseInn.com Website: www.masonhouseinn.com

KANSAS
WHERE TO VISIT

★ ★ ★ ★ ★ ★

THE HAUNTED TOWN OF ATCHISON, KANSAS

Individuals who have visited this town have claimed a wide assortment of ghostly sightings, and a variety of other unexplained happenings.

The Gargoyle Home, originally known as the "Waggener House," is believed to be one of the most known haunted houses in the ghost town. Built in 1885, there was a lawyer named B.P Waggener, and the gargoyle statutes there were believed to have been a representation of his deal with the Devil.

The gift shop is full of Haunted Atchison products, as well as Amelia Earhart memorabilia, railroad history items, and much more. The staff can help you with directions and information about their unique shops and spectacular eateries.

Santa Fe Depot is the tourist center and gift shop. The staff are friendly and welcome tourism.

THE HAUNTED TOWN OF ATCHISON KANSAS
200 S. 10th Street, Atchison, KS 66002
Phone: (800) 234-185 Email: tours@atchisonkansas.net
Website: http://www.atchisonkansas.net/HauntedAtchison/home.html

KENTUCKY

★★★ WHERE TO VISIT ★★★

THE GHOST HUNTER SHOP

Scarefest. The author with Ernie Hudson of *The Crow* and *Ghostbusters*. Patti Star founded Scarefest and runs the shop for the convention during the event, but also operates the Ghosthunter Shop all year round for tourists and locals alike who want anything from books on spirits to EVP meters! *Photograph courtesy of the author*

If you happen to be in Lexington, home of the Midwest's largest horror convention, stop by the Ghost Hunter Shop, run by the delightful lady who heads the convention, Patti Starr, author of *Ghosthunting, Kentucky*. Here is where you can shop for all your ghost hunting needs in Lexington's one and only premiere ghost hunter store, providing you with equipment, books, vests, CDs, DVDs, EMF meters, infrared thermometers, dowsing tools, and so much more. You will receive a free copy of *Oracle 20/20 Magazine* (a $3.95 value) with your purchase, and you may purchase platinum tickets to the convention Scarefest. (If you happen to be in the area during the event, is it is well worth it to attend! You may even meet the authors of this book at the Dark Moon Press booth!)

THE GHOST HUNTER SHOP
835 Porter Place, Lexington, KY 40508
Phone: (859) 576-5517 Email: patti@ghosthunter.com
Website: http://www.ghosthuntershop.com/

Store hours are Monday through Friday, 10 a.m. to 5 p.m. Saturday, Sunday, or after hours by appointment only.

THE
WAVERLY HILLS SANATORIUM

The Waverly Hills Sanatorium.
Photograph courtesy Tim Shaw

Waverly Hills Sanatorium, located in Louisville, Kentucky, is owned by Charlie and Tina Mattingly and The Waverly Hills Historical Society. It is said to be one of the most haunted places in the country, with a death tally as high as 64,000 patients who were ravaged by a deadly disease commonly referred to as the "white death," or tuberculosis, which quickly wiped out entire towns. In 1926, a hospital was constructed on a windswept hill in southern Jefferson County that was designed to combat this horrific disease; however, it was poorly chosen to be constructed on swampland. It did nothing but increase the disease, despite the fact it was considered the most advanced hospital of its kind in the world. Still, at the time, not much was known about tuberculosis and how to treat it, so a lot of the treatments were experimental.

The majority of patients left through what came to be known as the "body chute," which was a tunnel that led from the hospital to railroad tracks, allowing for discreet corpse disposal. This elaborate system was a motorized rail and cable system, by which the bodies were lowered in secret to the waiting trains at the bottom of the hill, so that patients would not see it and become demoralized.

Various methods were used as treatments. One consisted of having the lungs exposed to ultraviolet light to try to stop the spread of the disease. This took place in "sun rooms" on the roof or open porches of the hospital. Combined with the belief that fresh air was thought to also be the cure, patients were often placed out on open porches—photographs of the era show patients lounging in chairs, covered with snow. Another even worse treatment, described as a "last resort," was ghastly. The procedure involved implanting balloons into the lungs and then filling them with air to expand them. This happened after there were operations removing the patient's muscles and ribs in order to allow the lungs to expand further and let in more oxygen.

Budget cuts from the 1960s to the 1970s led to both horrible conditions and patient mistreatments, and by 1982, the state closed the facility. The buildings and property were auctioned off and changed ownership repeatedly over the next several decades.

As time passed, Waverly Hills attracted both the homeless seeking shelter, and juvenile delinquents, who broke in and started rumors of Waverly Hills being haunted by ghosts. The stories speak of a hearse that appears at the back of the building dropping off coffins, a woman with bleeding wrists who cries for help, and others. It is said, depending on who is speaking, that a ghostly child haunts the third floor, as people report

having heard a ball bouncing on the floor and down the stairs, and of faint voices of children chanting the poem "Ring around the rosie" up on the roof.

Waverly is also famous for the story of two nurses who committed suicide while there. In 1928, the head nurse in Room 502 was found dead after hanging herself from the light fixture. In 1932, another nurse who worked in Room 502 was said to have jumped from the roof patio, plunging several stories to her death. My friend, author and medium Reverend Tim Shaw, visited Waverly several times and told me of people who saw her full-body apparition on the fifth floor, and that ghost researchers are drawn to the two nurses' stations near where they committed suicide. Tim told me that the door showing cuts into it came from an ax when it would not open, yet later it pushed open with barely a turn. The investigator standing in the open room claimed he was scratched by something that marked his side, though no one saw him near anything at the time that could have resulted in this injury.

The Louisville Ghost Hunters Society presented the hospital to a national television audience, holding two ghost conferences at Waverly. Fox Television's *World's Scariest Places* presented the group's hot spots, and where spirits could be felt.

THE WAVERLY HILLS SANATORIUM
4400 Paralee Lane, Louisville, KY 40272 Tour Scheduling/Reservation: (502) 933-2142
Email: info@therealwaverlyhills.com Website: http://therealwaverlyhills.com/

Office hours, reservations and scheduling:

Monday, Tuesday, Thursday, and Friday open at 9 a.m. Lunch from 1 p.m. to 2 p.m. Closed at 5 p.m.; Wednesday open at 9 a.m., closed at 1 p.m.

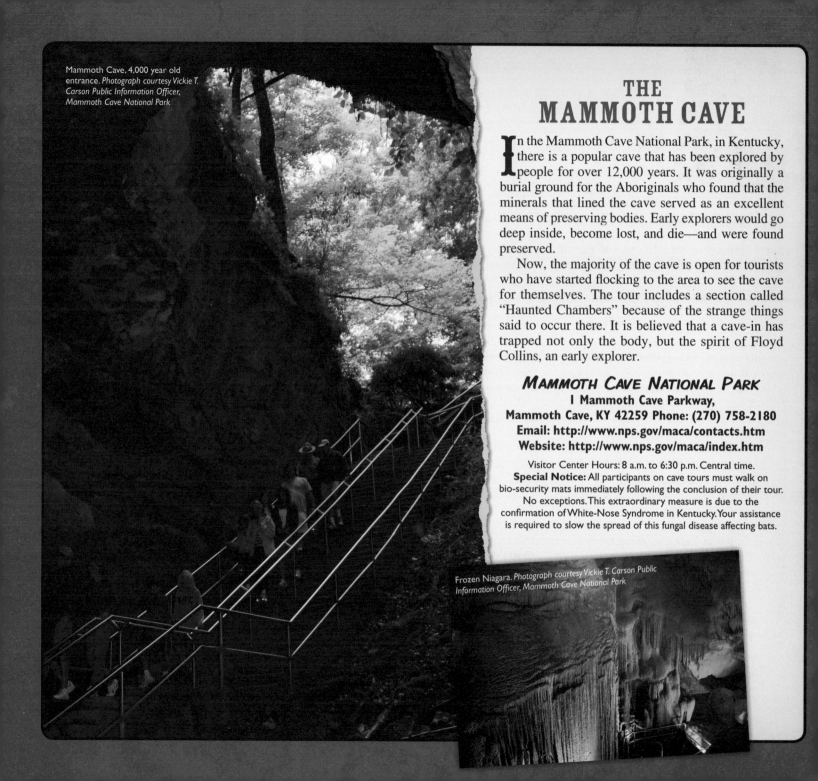

Mammoth Cave, 4,000 year old entrance. *Photograph courtesy Vickie T. Carson Public Information Officer, Mammoth Cave National Park*

THE MAMMOTH CAVE

In the Mammoth Cave National Park, in Kentucky, there is a popular cave that has been explored by people for over 12,000 years. It was originally a burial ground for the Aboriginals who found that the minerals that lined the cave served as an excellent means of preserving bodies. Early explorers would go deep inside, become lost, and die—and were found preserved.

Now, the majority of the cave is open for tourists who have started flocking to the area to see the cave for themselves. The tour includes a section called "Haunted Chambers" because of the strange things said to occur there. It is believed that a cave-in has trapped not only the body, but the spirit of Floyd Collins, an early explorer.

MAMMOTH CAVE NATIONAL PARK
**1 Mammoth Cave Parkway,
Mammoth Cave, KY 42259 Phone: (270) 758-2180
Email: http://www.nps.gov/maca/contacts.htm
Website: http://www.nps.gov/maca/index.htm**

Visitor Center Hours: 8 a.m. to 6:30 p.m. Central time.
Special Notice: All participants on cave tours must walk on bio-security mats immediately following the conclusion of their tour. No exceptions. This extraordinary measure is due to the confirmation of White-Nose Syndrome in Kentucky. Your assistance is required to slow the spread of this fungal disease affecting bats.

Frozen Niagara. *Photograph courtesy Vickie T. Carson Public Information Officer, Mammoth Cave National Park*

"WELCOME TO........ Bobby Mackey's ENJOY YOUR EVENING"

BOBBY MACKEY'S MUSIC WORLD

In the city of Wilder is the famous Bobby Mackey's Music World, also known as "Hell's Gate." Today, this building is a popular nightclub for country music. In the 1800s, it was a slaughterhouse for forty years. Many believe Bobby Mackey's Music World is one of the most haunted places in Kentucky.

In the late 1800s, the building was abandoned and researchers suggest that an occult group used the area for rituals. Local authorities found fresh blood in the basement area, and remains of animals that were believed to have been sacrificed there.

By the year of 1896, a lady by the name of Pearl Bryan had been murdered. One of the cult members was a medical student at the time and apparently believed that he could do an abortion on her, using dental tools and cocaine. Despite his best efforts, it failed, and in desperation, he actually beheaded her.

He was sentenced to death. Eventually, a new owner by the name of Brady took over and had plans to turn the building into a casino. Mobsters scared him out of the place, though, and he committed suicide in 1965.

Eventually, Janet Mackey and her husband, Bobby Mackey, purchased the building and opened Bobby Mackey's Music World. The initial caretaker said he noticed lights turning on after he had turned them off, strange and unusual sounds, as well as a woman's spirit that may or may not be the murdered woman.

BOBBY MACKEY'S MUSIC WORLD
44 Licking Pike, Wilder, KY 41071
Phone: (859) 431-5588 Website: www.bobbymackey.com/

WHERE TO STAY

JAILER'S INN
BED & BREAKFAST

Jailer's Inn is a haunted bed and breakfast in Bardstown, Kentucky. Originally, since 1797, it was a jail, until the year 1987 when it was transformed into the B&B. The Travel Channel listed it as one of the "Ten Most Haunted Places in the United States," due to several hauntings visitors have said they experienced. Before it was a bed and breakfast, the location was a jail for 200 years. While being held at the jail, many people died due to sickness or they were murdered in their cells; that might be part of the reasoning for the haunts there now.

One of the most popular hauntings at the bed and breakfast is a ghostly female who is believed to be one of the original jailers. Her name was Ms. Mckay, and her husband initially started as the jailer of the facility, but she took over after his death.

One of the most congested areas of ghostly presences is known as the "courtyard," where hangings took place.

JAILER'S INN BED AND BREAKFAST
111 West Stephen Foster Avenue, Bardstown, KY 40004
Phone: (800) 948-5551 Email: cpaul@jailersinn.com Website: http://www.jailersinn.com/

Rooms range from $80 to $145, in various different styles.
Some of the rooms are old Victorian, and one of them is fashioned into an old jail cell. Tours are offered daily.

LOUISIANA

WHERE TO VISIT

★ ★ ★   ★ ★ ★

NEW ORLEANS

THE CITY OF NEW ORLEANS TIES SAINT AUGUSTINE AS THE MOST HAUNTED CITY IN THE UNITED STATES.

VOODOO MUSEUM

The New Orleans Historic Voodoo Museum, which lies in the heart of the New Orleans French Quarter, is one of the most unique, and interesting, small museums in the country. A fixture in New Orleans since 1972, it exists to preserve the legacy of New Orleans' Voodoo history and culture, while educating and entertaining the visitor about all the secrets of Voodoo, the history and folklore of rituals, zombies, gris-gris, and more. When speaking to the owner of the museum, he made mention that his establishment was featured on The History Channel.

VOODOO MUSEUM
724 Dumaine Street, New Orleans, LA 70116
Phone: (504) 680-0128, Website: http://www.voodoomuseum.com/

Open seven days a week from 10 a.m. to 6 p.m. (or later). The museum is located in the Garden District (Washington Avenue and Prytania) section of New Orleans and accessible by the St. Charles Avenue streetcar, and between Bourbon and Royal Streets.

New Orleans LaLaurie Mansion.
Photograph courtesy Library of Congress

LALAURIE MANSION

LaLaurie Mansion was owned by Madame Delphine LaLaurie and her husband, Dr. Louis LaLaurie, a socialite of great wealth and prominence in the city of New Orleans in the 1830s. Elaborate parties would be hosted at the house. In 1834, a fire broke out in the mansion, and when help arrived, a horrific scene was found in a hidden room. They discovered tortured and abused slaves who worked in the house. Brad Steiger, author of *Real Zombies*, *The Living Dead*, and *Creatures of the Apocalypse* describes in his books the horrendous experiments that were conducted there on living people. Some slaves were kept in cages or bound to operating tables in various stages of dissection while still alive. Delphine fled the fire, and both she and the doctor were never seen again.

The home has undergone many changes and owners over the years, with one of the most recent owners being actor Nicolas Cage. Cage said of the LaLaurie house, "You know, other people have beachfront property; I have ghost-front property." Unfortunately, Cage lost the property in a foreclosure auction.

LaLaurie Mansion
1140 Royal Street (From Edmond Soniat du Fossat)
New Orleans, LA 70116

NEW ORLEANS' VOODOO CEMETERY GATES OF GUINEE

Also known by locals as "The Portal To The Afterworld," this Voodoo cemetery is named after Ghede, the wise man, for his knowledge is an accumulation of the knowledge of all of the deceased. He stands at the center of all the roads that lead to Guinee, the Afterworld. New Orleans tour guides for the haunted cemetery will skirt around the issue. The older people who know about Voodoo say that only someone pure of heart, with only one burning question to be answered by the dead, is ever told the whole truth about the portal and its real location. An unnamed New Orleans Voodoo priestess says quite bluntly, "Search and you shall find them [the gates of the portal that leads to the dead] rusted shut, or worse, they will certainly find you and be wide and opened." However, you may just find someone in the local occult shops who would be willing to help you!

Gates of Guinee

The exact location of the Gates of Guinee vary among Voodoo practitioners. Some see the seven gates as a metaphor for the seven days after death. Some say it is the Cemetery No. 1, and still others whisper that it is at the Canal Street crossroads and Basin Street. We dare our readers to discover its true whereabouts!

Lafayette Cemetery No. 1.
Photograph courtesy Judi Bottoni for
Save Our Cemeteries ©2008

CITY OF THE DEAD LAFAYETTE CEMETERY NO. 1

Lafayette No. 1 is the cemetery most often used in films made in New Orleans. The oldest city burial site since 1833, Lafayette Cemetery No. 1 is placed on the National Register of Historic Places by virtue of its significant history, location, and architectural importance. Built in 1833, by 1852, the cemetery was filled to capacity when almost 2,000 yellow fever victims were buried. Today, many tombs are sinking into the ground.

There are those who say that this is the most haunted cemetery. Indeed, this decaying, grand location stirred the imagination of local author Anne Rice, who has used the place in many of her books. She even staged a mock funeral here, to launch the publication of *Memnoch the Devil*; she herself was the corpse, wearing an antique wedding dress in an open coffin carried by pall bearers. Her best-known title turned into film is *Interview with a Vampire,* filmed throughout the French Quarter and starring Tom Cruise, Brad Pitt, and Kirsten Dunst. Legions of Voodoo practitioners

make their way through the City of the Dead to visit the grave of Voodoo high priestess Marie Laveau who was buried here; and for generations, the devoted and the curious have been visiting this site, conducting rituals, and leaving all kinds of gris-gris. Gris-gris, according to my friends who study Voodoo and Hodoo, are small items of the Afro -Caribbean religion, used for luck and to ward off evil from befalling the owner.

Marie Laveau, born to a wealthy French planter, and a mother who some say could have been a mulatto slave, was a Caribbean Voodoo practitioner. She used theatrics and wealth to rise to the top of the city's most colorful and sought-out celebrity, using theatrical staging to put on performances. Her general Voodoo practice became highly lucrative.

In Haunted Places: The National Directory, Hauck (1996) writes of Marie: "Her ghost and those of her followers are said to practice wild Voodoo rituals in her old house."

CITY OF THE DEAD, LAFAYETTE CEMETERY NO. 1
1400 Washington Avenue, Garden District, New Orleans, LA 70130
For information, call (888) 721-7493 Website: http://www.nolacemeteries.com/lafayette1.html

Lafayette Cemetery No. 1.
Photograph courtesy Judi Bottoni for
Save Our Cemeteries ©2008

MAINE

WHERE TO VISIT

★ ★ ★ ★ ★ ★

ROUTE 2A

There is a rural section of road in northern Maine off of U.S. Route 2, called Route 2A, running through what is known as the Haynesville Woods, near the town of Haynesville in southern Aroostook County.

The locals talk about a young lady who has been seen suddenly appearing out of nowhere in front of a vehicle. Those who have picked her up say that when they near the end of the woods, she vanishes. According to legend, this woman was newly married and traveling with her husband down that same road when the vehicle they were in struck a utility pole, killing her husband instantly. Though the woman managed to free herself from the vehicle, she perished laying in the snow and the freezing cold weather.

The other most commonly mentioned spirit along this stretch of road is the ghost of a young girl who was killed by a tractor trailer as she walked along Route 2 in 1967. Whether or not this is true, we don't recommend you travel this route by dark!

ROUTE 2A
Haynesville Woods area Southern Aroostook County

WHERE TO STAY

★ ★ ★ ★ ★ ★

THE
KENNEBUNK INN

Built in the year of 1799, this inn is considered to be highly haunted, according to individuals who work there and others who have visited. It is said that spirits who lingered in the establishment are unhappy about the additions to the place and make it clear to visitors. One story is of a waiter who was carrying a tray of wine to some of the guests. Slowly, a glass of wine rose off of the tray and flew into the air, only to suddenly and violently be thrown to the floor.

KENNEBUNK INN
45 Main Street, Kennebunk, ME 04043
Phone: (207) 985-3351 Website: www.thekennebunkinn.com/

Rates at the time of this publication are $164 per night.

MARYLAND

★ ★ ★ WHERE TO VISIT ★ ★ ★

OLD WESTERN BURIAL GROUND

It is rumored that the Old Western Burial Ground, a graveyard in Baltimore known as the "Presbyterian Churchyard," is haunted. Yet even if this were not the case, it certainly is noteworthy to visit, as Edgar Allan Poe is buried there.

Located just below Westminster Hall (also believed to be haunted), lies the cemetery often referred to as one of the most haunted places in America. There are stories that many individuals were buried in the cemetery who were not dead, and now they seek out those responsible for their deaths for revenge.

The "Skull of Cambridge" is buried here. A murdered minister, as the story goes, was removed from his grave and his skull placed in cement in order to block out the sounds of screams that people claim came from it. It is said that several people experienced insanity and then were placed in psychiatric wards after being exposed to the skull.

OLD WESTERN BURIAL GROUND
519 W. Fayette Street
Baltimore, MD 21201
Phone: (410) 706-2072
Website: http://www.westminsterhall.org/

Edgar Allan Poe Museum. *Photograph courtesy Library of Congress*

EDGAR ALLAN POE MUSEUM

Over 160 years after his death, Edgar Allan Poe's home has been turned into a place for fans to visit. To be so fondly remembered by many would seem ironic, as during his life, he was not hailed in such a way. He was known more for being found in a tavern, delirious and in mourning two years after the death of his young wife, Virginia.

His home, now a museum, is still open as of this research; however, the city of Baltimore has cut off its $85,000 in annual support for two years in a row (2011 and 2012),not choosing to subsidize a museum where the impoverished Poe lived from around 1833 to 1835. The house has been operating on reserve funds, which are expected to run dry in a year. "It would be ironic, after all these years of aggressively and actively promoting the Poe House and the Poe grave, that we may have to close it," said Jeff Jerome, the house's curator for more than thirty years. He said that to switch to self-supporting is impractical, given that the house generates only a small amount of revenue from admissions, special events, and the sale of books and T-shirts from its 5,000 visitors a year. Notable visitors include author Stephen King and actor Vincent Price, who Mr. Jerome said visited the house some years ago, commenting, "This house, gives me the creeps."

A number of pieces related to Poe are exhibited, including the traveling desk he used at the University of Virginia and a full-sized color reproduction of the only known portrait of Poe's wife, Virginia, completed at the time of her death in 1847. A set of Gustave Dore's 1884 illustrations for Poe's *The Raven* can be seen on the second floor. With media exposure, donations, and a television show based on Poe's life, it may yet withstand the test of time.

THE POE MUSEUM
203 North Amity Street, Baltimore, MD 21223-2501
Phone: (410) 396-7932
Website: www.poemuseum.org

The USS Constellation.
Photograph courtesy Library of Congress

THE
USS CONSTELLATION

Baltimore, Maryland is quite an interesting tourist location for the history buff and ghost hunter alike. Docked at Pier 1 in Baltimore's Inner Harbor is a massive fighting ship that saw service for nearly a century and a half, (in use from the Civil War to the end of World War II). The USS *Constellation* continues to draw in many visitors who report seeing what they believe to be "apparitions," and claim that they are wearing clothing that looks much like that worn in the early 18th century—long before the ship was actually built. Historians who believe in apparitions say these ghosts seem to be from two ships that emerged prior to the USS *Constellation,* known as the USS *Constitution. A*s years passed, many soldiers died while protecting their country. Today, many people visit the USS *Constellation* to pay their respects to those who served.

One of the spirits rumored to haunt this massive ship is Captain Thomas Truxtun. It is said that this particular spirit thanked officials of the ship for the tour and commented on how helpful the tour guide was. Another is the spirit that appears to be a teenage boy. This particular boy looks too young to have served as a soldier, but many believe him to have been a "Powder Boy" on the USS *Constellation*, brought on ship in order to carry gunpowder to the soldiers. These boys were referred to as "Powder Monkeys" during the war. It is believed that one of these boys, in the 1800s, was the victim of murder. To this day, individuals claim to see the apparition screaming and struggling.

As haunted ships go, the USS *Constellation* is well worth the visit!

USS CONSTELLATION
301 East Pratt Street, Pier 1, Baltimore, MD 21202
Phone: (410) 539-1797 Website: http://www.history.navy.mil/ussconstitution/

The USS *Constellation* is open to the public, and for a fee, one may tour. Current entrance fee: admission (including audio tour) $8.75 adults, $7.50 seniors, $4.75 children 6-14. The ship will be closed on Martin Luther King, Jr's birthday, President's Day, Thanksgiving Day, Christmas Day, and New Year's Day. Please arrive at least 15 minutes early to allow time for security screening, which is required for all visitors. November 1 to March 31, Thursday to Sunday, 10 a.m. to 4 p.m. April 1 to September 30, Tuesday to Sunday, 10 a.m. to 6 p.m. October 1 to October 31, Tuesday to Sunday, 10 a.m. to 4 p.m.

POINT LOOKOUT
LIGHTHOUSE

This structure has become an attraction to paranormal researchers around the world. Located in Scotland, Maryland, this particular lighthouse became operational in the year 1830.

Commonly referred to as "Point Lookout State Park," the lighthouse is said to have a "grisly history" compared to other state parks in the country. The government constructed what was known as "Hammond General Hospital" during the Civil War, and it was used to treat soldiers who fought and held a storage area for casualties for the North. Eventually, a camp that would be used as a prison was established on the grounds so that an area for soldiers of the confederacy at times reached 20,000 detainees!

A large number of hauntings that are said to occur at the Lighthouse are reported by visitors and employees who have heard voices. One investigator documented a voice that was caught on tape saying, "Fire if they get too close."

A female apparition, Ann Davis, has been seen at the top section of the stairs, and in many places at the Point Lookout Lighthouse immense temperature drops have been reported.

POINT LOOKOUT STATE PARK
11175 Point Lookout Road, Scotland, MD 20687
Phone (301) 872-5699 Website: www.ptlookoutlighthouse.com

MASSACHUSETTS

WHERE TO VISIT

SALEM WITCH MUSEUM

...m Witch Museum,
...ecca Nurse. Photograph
...rtesy Tina Jordan Director of
Salem Witch Museum

I remember my first visit to the Salem Witch Museum when I was a young child. At the time, I was attending a private religious school back home and was visiting with my grandparents in Boston. My father decided to take my brother and me to the museum. I had never been more terrified by anything in my life up to that point. Now, I find such a place a treasure, teaching people the history of such an unfortunate event.

The museum brings us back to important incidents in the evolution of our nation. While we now value religious freedom and diversity in our country, it has not always been that way. The people who settled Massachusetts for purposes of religious freedom had very little tolerance for anything other than their own viewpoints.

The year 1692 is an important one for the museum. By the summer of that year, 180 people had been accused of witchcraft and imprisoned. Bridget Bishop, the first of the victims, was tried on June 2 and hung eight days later. That summer would see much more of this happening.

The museum makes this time from our past come to life, using stage sets with life-size figures—the same life-size figures that scared me so much as a young child, but that I appreciate now as an adult.

The museum also has an outstanding gift shop with some great items you can't find just anywhere.

While visiting the museum, be sure to spend time in Salem itself. The city now celebrates its past, and even has a statue of Samantha from the hit television show *Bewitched*.

SALEM WITCH MUSEUM
Washington Square, Salem, MA 01970
Phone: (978) 744-1692 Website: http://www.salemwitchmuseum.com/
10 a.m. to 5 p.m. daily; 10 a.m. to 7 p.m. July/August. Closed on Thanksgiving, Christmas, and New Year's Day.

Salem Witch Museum, Magic Circle.
Photograph courtesy Tina Jordan
Director of the Salem Witch Museum

Hammond castle. *Photograph courtesy public domain, taken by Dale E. Martin*

Hammond castle, Great Hall. *Photograph public domain taken by Dale E. Martin*

HAMMOND CASTLE

On April 13, 1888, John Hays Hammond, Jr. was born in San Francisco, California. Later, while in Europe, he developed a fascination with castles.

In the year 1926, Hammond began construction on the infamous Hammond Castle. He constructed it in a unique style, with sections designed to highlight various distinguished periods of architecture that were popular in Europe, including Romanesque, Medieval, Renaissance French, and Gothic. In addition to this, he added secret passages.

In 1965, Hammond passed away and was buried on the property in the same location as his beloved cat. He specified that, in death, he wanted the grounds in which he would be buried to be covered with poison ivy. He did not want to be bothered once he was put to rest.

But over the years, many have claimed to have seen his ghost around the premises. In addition, it is believed that the deceased wife of Mr. Hammond still moves among the castle rooms.

HAMMOND CASTLE MUSEUM
80 Hesperus Avenue, Gloucester, MA 01930 Phone: (978) 283-2080
Website: http://www.hammondcastle.org

If you are interested in the paranormal, there are self-guided tours that can be taken at the haunted Hammond Castle. Saturdays and Sundays from 10 a.m. to 4 p.m. with the last ticket sold at 3:30 p.m. The castle will be open additional days a week after June 2013. Admission fees are $10 for adults, $8 for seniors (65 and older), and $6 for children (ages 6-12).

★ ★ ★ WHERE TO STAY ★ ★ ★

THE
LIZZIE BORDEN BED & BREAKFAST

This historical home is the location of the murders of Andrew and Abby Borden, who died by being struck repeatedly with an ax on the morning of August 4, 1892. Lizzie Borden, the daughter of Andrew and stepdaughter of Abby, became the prime suspect and the subject of a popular children's rhyme.

Lizzie Borden took an axe,
And gave her mother forty whacks,
When she saw what she had done,
She gave her father forty-one.

Reportedly, the Bordens were not a loving family unit, and on that day in 1892, the wealthy businessman and his wife were found brutally murdered. It was the trial of the century, as their daughter, Lizzie, was indicted for the crime, only to be acquitted by a jury. She and her sister eventually moved to a home on French Street, and the murder home is now a bed-and-breakfast where Andrew and Abby are said to still roam.

This beautifully restored Greek-revival home has also been filmed by the SCARED! film crew, led by the company owner, Brian J. Cano.

The Lizzie Borden bed and breakfast.
Photograph courtesy Brian J. Cano

LIZZIE BORDEN BED & BREAKFAST
230 Second Street, Fall River, MA 02721
Phone: (508) 675-7333 Website: http://www.lizzie-borden.com/

HAWTHORNE HOTEL

In Salem, there is a hotel that is believed to be haunted known as the Hawthorne Hotel, named after the famous author, Nathaniel Hawthorne. Hawthorne is often called the "Son of Salem," best known for his novel, *The Scarlett Letter*, which was written in the year 1850. In the early 1900s, the individuals in Salem saw a need to have a hotel for those traveling through the city, and thus the hotel was built. The Hawthorne Hotel has been seen in numerous television shows, such as *Bewitched*, and the Syfy channel program, *Ghost Hunters*.

This land was once an apple orchard owned by Bridget Bishop, the first individual to be hanged at "Gallows Hill" after being convicted of practicing witchcraft during the "Salem Witch Trials." To this day, when you go to the hotel, you can smell apples, despite the fact that now the orchards no longer exist.

Over the years, there have been many reports of paranormal activity within the hotel. Guests have reported strange things happening in room 325 and 612, such as water and lights turning on by themselves, and there are claims of an apparition that appears to be a woman.

Hawthorne Hotel
18 Washington Square W., Salem, MA 01970
Phone: (978) 744-4080 and (1-800) 729-7829
Email: info@hawthornehotel.com
Website: http://www.hawthornehotel.com/

Seul Choix Lighthouse.
Photograph courtesy
Library of Congress

MICHIGAN

★ ★ ★ WHERE TO VISIT ★ ★ ★

THE SEUL CHOIX LIGHTHOUSE

Located near Gulliver, at the northern point of Lake Michigan, this area is said to be one of the most haunted locations in the area of the Great Lakes. The Seul Choix Lighthouse continues to interest paranormal investigators, due in part because over two dozen ships have wrecked in the waters causing 500 deaths.

In 1892, the lighthouse was constructed and in use until 1910, when Joseph Willie Townsend, the caretaker, passed away. He was known to enjoy smoking cigars and paranormal investigators say they can still smell burning cigars.

Many individuals have witnessed what they believe to be the ghost of Joseph Townsend.

SEUL CHOIX LIGHTHOUSE
672 North West Gulliver Lake Road, Gulliver, MI 49840
Phone: 906-283-3183 Website: www.haunted-places-to-go.com/haunted-lighthouse.html

THE
FELT MANSION

The Felt Mansion is considered to be one of the haunted places in Michigan, and whether or not this is true, it is an amazing endeavor for its time because it was completed during the Great Depression. Construction began in the year 1925, with a huge 17,000-square-foot living space. On the third floor of the home was a majestic ballroom.

Dorr E. Felt was an inventor who wanted to have a lavish, summer home for his wife, Agnes. Dorr was a prodigy when it came to mechanics.

Approximately a month and a half after the home was finished, Agnes Felt passed away. Dorr himself died about one year and six months later. Then the mansion was sold and became a Catholic prep school until the end of the 1970s, when the state of Michigan decided to purchase the property and convert it into a prison. Today, the prison is gone and workers are trying to restore the mansion to its original state.

Ghost hunters will love this place, as it is rumored to be hunted by the couple. Fans of architecture of days gone by will marvel at the beauty as it is restored.

THE FELT ESTATE
6597 138th Avenue, Holland, MI 49423
Phone: 616.335.3050 http://www.feltmanslon.org/toursandevents.html

LANDMARK INN

The of the city of Marquette in the state of Michigan began back in the year 1910. This fabulous Inn itself did not open until January 8, 1930, and it was the crown jewel of the area. Film noir history fans will love the splendor and history.

Amelia Earhart visited the Landmark Inn in 1932. Amelia, the female aviator who disappeared across the ocean during her voyage and was never seen again—but is now seen here in room 502.

Also of note, comedians Abbott and Costello stayed at the establishment, as has Jim Harrison, Maya Angelou, Bill Cosby, and many others.

A murder is said to have occurred at the Inn. A man murdered a woman when he discovered that she was sleeping around on him. He took her body to the basement area of the structure and left her there. The crew working to complete this area often report hearing the crying and faint whispers of a female voice.

Landmark Inn
230 North Front Street, Marquette Township, MI 49855
Phone: (906) 228-2580 Website: www.thelandmarkinn.com/

Minnesota Science Museum Science Museum. *Photograph courtesy of the Science Museum of Minnesota*

MINNESOTA

WHERE TO VISIT

THE
MUSEUM OF QUESTIONABLE
MEDICAL DEVICES

PSYCOGRAPH

Minnesota Science Museum Psycograph. *Photograph courtesy of the Science Museum of Minnesota*

Invented by Henry Lavery in the 1930s, the Psycograph was designed to read the bumps on a patient's head and measure the strength of their personality traits. An operator adjusted the 32-prong headpiece upon a patient's head and the Psycograph generated a report, ranking the talents and personality characteristics, based on the size and shape of the patient's skull.

On the Psycograph scale, a score of 1 indicated that a patient was deficient in that area, and a score of 5 indicated a superior standing. "Experts" used these scores to help patients build upon their character traits. The scores even helped patients select careers deemed suitable to their personality strengths!

The Museum of Questionable Medical Devices is also known as the "Quackery Hall of Fame" located at the Science Museum of Minnesota. Founder Bob McCoy retired and closed the St. Anthony Main location of the museum in 2002, donating his devices to the Science Museum. Pieces displayed include the Prostate Gland Warmer, which is actually just a four-inch probe with a blue light bulb at the end, a "rejuvenator" that uses magnetism, radio waves, infra-red, and ultra-violet rays. The Science Museum of Minnesota's Questionable Medical Devices display gives visitors a peek at machines from the past 100 years that were designed to "cure" what ails the average human. In some cases, these failed remedies were honest mistakes, but many others were deliberate frauds. Numerous devices can be found in the museum, such as the Kellogg Vibratory Chair, bloodletting devices, and many that work to this date. Most are also featured in McCoy's book, *Quack! Tales of Medical Fraud from the Museum of Questionable Medical Devices.*

Sarah Imholte, the PR Coordinator for the Science Museum of Minnesota describes two such devices as seen in these photos.

THE MUSEUM OF QUESTIONABLE MEDICAL DEVICES
120 W. Kellogg Boulevard, Fl 3, Saint Paul, MN 55102
Phone: (651) 221-9444 Website: museumofquackery.com

Hours: Tuesday to Wednesday, Sunday 9:30 a.m. to 5 p.m.
Thursday to Saturday 9:30 a.m. to 9 p.m.

Minnesota Science Museum Kellogg Vibratory Chair. *Photograph courtesy of the Science Museum of Minnesota*

KELLOGG VIBRATORY CHAIR

Invented by John Harvey Kellogg, the Kellogg Vibratory Chair was commonly used in sanitariums to treat patients around 1900. Powered by electricity, the chair shook and rattled loudly. Patients held onto the side handles to keep from being jostled too much. With its violent vibrations, the Kellogg Vibratory Chair was reputed to cure constipation and improve respiration.

WHERE TO STAY

THE
PALMER HOUSE HOTEL

The Palmer House Hotel is located in Sauk Centre, Minnesota. In 1900, in the month of June, the structure caught fire and was destroyed. A man by the name of R.L. Palmer decided to rebuild the hotel and finished in the year 1901. At this point, he named the hotel The Palmer House.

By the year 1974, the ownership of the hotel had exchanged hands, and visitors and workers now claim it to be haunted. Several guests have heard knocks that seem to emerge from within the walls of their rooms. There are many different types of unexplained phenomenon within the structure; two of the hauntings were thought to be due to suicides.

THE PALMER HOUSE HOTEL
Sinclair Lewis Avenue, Sauk Centre, MN 56378
Phone: (320) 351-9100 Website: http://www.thepalmerhousehotel.com/

MISSISSIPPI

WHERE TO VISIT

THE DELTA QUEEN

The *Delta Queen* is considered to be one of the most haunted ships. This ship took its first voyage in 1927, and still travels the Mississippi and Ohio Rivers.

Mary B. Greene, "Ma Greene," was one of the founders of the *Delta Queen* Steamboat Company, as well as being the first female captain of the ship. She was known to hold very strong opinions against alcohol on her ship.

In 1949, Ma Greene passed away, and shortly after that, a group decided to set up a saloon on the *Delta Queen*. The first cocktail was served onboard the American riverboat, and just minutes afterwards, a barge unexpectedly ran into them, completely destroying the saloon. Oddly enough, the barge was named after Ma Greene, called "Captain Mary B." Since then, many have claimed to have seen an apparition that resembles the former captain who is watching over the *Delta Queen*.

THE DELTA QUEEN
100 River Street, Chattanooga, TN 37405
Phone: For reservations, (800) 434-1232 Website: www.deltaqueenhotel.net

MCRAVEN HOME

Reputed to be the most haunted house in all of Mississippi, "The McRaven Home" was built in 1797 by Andrew Glass, and during the Civil War, fell victim to the bullets and cannons. At that time, it was known as the infamous "Bobb House" on the street called McRaven. Eventually, this structure would come to be known as the McRaven Home, even though the street was changed to Harrison Street.

During the war, several individuals died in and around the property of the home, one being a sergeant who was looting and died due to a brick blow to the head. The house was eventually purchased by a family named Murray in 1882.

The hauntings of the McRaven Home include that of Mary Elizabeth Howard, who lived in the structure in the early days. While there, she gave birth and also died in the home. Locals say she turns the light in a room on and off. The home served as a hospital during the Civil War and the fallen soldiers are said to linger the grounds as well.

The McRaven Home now offers tours to the public, and has been featured on A&E TV, The Travel Channel, History Channel, and Discovery Channel.

THE MCRAVEN HOME
1445 Harrison Street, Vicksburg, MS 39180
Phone: (601) 636-1663 (Leonard Fuller)
Website: www.mcraventourhome.com/

Tour schedule: fall and spring hours 9 a.m. to 5 p.m. daily. Sunday 10 a.m. to 5 p.m.
Summer starting June, ending Labor Day weekend 9 a.m. to 5 p.m. daily. Sunday 10 a.m. to 5 p.m.

CEDAR GROVE MANSION INN & RESTAURANT

Cedar Grove Mansion Inn and Restaurant is one of the largest and most elegant bed and breakfasts in the entire South. Located on five acres of gardens, this historic mansion attracts visitors who come to experience the paranormal activity that is believed to occur here.

There were several graves located on the property when it was purchased. It was believed that they belonged to the children of the founders, the Klein family. Two of the children were infants and passed away due to "crib death," and one is believed to be a teenage son who was accidentally shot. Many people who have visited the inn claim to hear infants crying, even when no children are listed as being there. Paranormal investigators believe that John and Elizabeth Klein still reside in the home in spirit. Both of these ghosts seem to enjoy the individuals who visit the mansion and often seem to be checking in on guests.

CEDAR GROVE MANSION INN & RESTAURANT
2200 Oak Street, Vicksburg, MS 39180
Phone: (601) 636-1000 Email: Info@CedarGroveInn.com
Website: www.cedargroveinn.com/

MISSOURI

WHERE TO VISIT

THE
HARNEY MANSION

This home was constructed in 1872 by a man named General William Harney. It served as a summer home for Harney from the year it was finished, in 1872, to 1884. Harney was a military figure who served in the Civil War and was well respected in the United States. Residing in the home until he sold the magnificent mansion, he then moved on to Florida.

The home changed hands several times, and during the 1990s, while renovations began on the structure, many different types of unexplained phenomenon started to occur, such as eerie glowing lights (captured on film) and there are reports from people who feel as if they have been touched while visiting.

THE HARNEY MANSION
332 South Mansion Street, Sullivan, MO 63080
Email: admin@paranormaltaskforce.com
Website: www.paranormaltaskforce.com/Harney.html

*FRIENDS OF GENERAL
HARNEY HOUSE, INC.*
P.O. Box 398, Sullivan, MI 63080

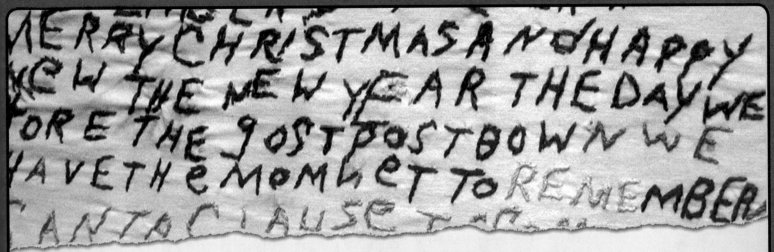

The Glore Psychiatric Museum embroidery detail of patient who communicated only by this means. *Photograph courtesy The Glore Psychiatric Museum*

THE
GLORE PSYCHIATRIC MUSEUM

The Glore Psychiatric Museum chronicles its 130-year history with full-sized replicas, interactive displays, artifacts, and documents that do a fantastic job describing the treatment in the past for mental illness. The museum is recognized as "one of the 50 most unusual museums in the country." It is also featured in the book, *1,000 Places to See Before You Die in the USA and Canada.*

The State Lunatic Asylum opened in November 1874 with twenty-five patients from the east of the city of St. Joseph. The hospital's first superintendent was Dr. Catlett. It reopened after a devastating fire in 1880 and became a sanctuary not only for the mentally ill, but also for tuberculosis, syphilitic, and alcoholic patients, as well as those with physical disabilities. But later, the asylum focused strictly on mental patients.

Renamed for its director, George Glore, in 1968, the founder spent most of his forty-one-year career with the Missouri Department of Mental Health, whose steadfast goal was to reduce the stigma associated with mentally handicapped patients. George Glore retired in 1996, but remained active with the Museum as an advisor, and until his death in 2010. During the last decade, the Museum has been the subject of various documentaries, including productions by The Learning Channel, The Discovery Channel, The PBS, Fox News, and The Science Channel.

The Glore Psychiatric Museum O'Halloran's Swing. *Photograph courtesy The Glore Psychiatric Museum*

THE GLORE PSYCHIATRIC MUSEUM
3406 Frederick Avenue, Saint Joseph, MO 64506
Phone: 1-816-232-8471 Email: sjm@stjosephmuseum.org
Website: www.stjosephmuseum.org

The Museum is one mile west of I-29, on Frederick Boulevard (exit 47). Hours are 10 a.m. to 5 p.m. Monday through Saturday and 1 to 5 p.m. on Sunday, closed on major holidays. Admission: $5.

The Glore Psychiatric Museum Trephination Exhibit. *Photograph courtesy The Glore Psychiatric Museum*

Bannack Ghost Town,
Montana. *Photograph courtesy
Library of Congress*

MONTANA

WHERE TO VISIT

BANNOCK GHOST TOWN

When gold was discovered in the small town Bannock, Montana, in 1862, prospectors filled the small city. Now, visitors to the Hotel Meade claim to encounter apparitions there, as well as at the hospital.

Dorothy Dunn is an individual that drowned in the creek near the town, and visitors feel as if she is still looking out one of the windows that are in one of the several buildings in this ghost town.

An employee told me about the infamous sheriff who was killed there, as well as the story of Henry Plumber, a man shot a hundred times, before his body was burned.

*BANNOCK GHOST TOWN
721 Bannack Road #2, Dillon, MT 59725-9300
Phone: (406) 834-3413 Email: bannack@smtel.com
Website: www.bannack.org*

NEBRASKA

WHERE TO VISIT

SPRINGFIELD, BALL CEMETERY

The Ball Cemetery in Nebraska originally opened as a cemetery designated for a family, then eventually opened to outsiders. One of the oldest graves to be located on the premises is marked with the year 1869; one among them is "Rattlesnake Pete," a friend of Old West criminals, such as "Buffalo Bill" and others. It is believed that this individual may still frequent the cemetery, looking for more of his friends. He is rumored to linger on the grounds and torment the people who visit the graves.

Many have visited here, taking pictures and videos of ghosts that show what could be apparitions.

SPRINGFIELD, BALL CEMETERY
20999 South 176th Street, Springfield, NE 68059
Website: http://www.interstateparanormal.net/ball.html

WHERE TO EAT

TRAILBLAZERS

This fine restaurant is located in a former Montgomery Ward building in the town's historic square. There is an excellent menu featuring the finest Nebraska corn-fed beef, chicken, and pork, as well as seafood and pasta dishes.

The restaurant is also purported to be haunted. There are rumors that Buffalo Bill Cody has some association with the restaurant. From many reports, it is said that something paranormal happens almost every day. If this is the case, there is a good chance that you will have an experience yourself, even if the experience is just a great meal in a great environment.

TRAILBLAZERS
500 4th Street, Fairbury, NE 68352
Phone: (402) 729-5205
Website: www.fairbury.com/pages/dining/trailblazers.html

NEVADA

WHERE TO VISIT

★ ★ ★ ★ ★ ★

THE JULIETTE C. RED LIGHT MUSEUM

If you would like to see the seedier side of American history, travel to Virginia City where you will find the nation's oldest known whorehouse that did a very steady business back during the days of the wild west. If you've been through the state of Nevada, you know that brothels are part and parcel to the history of the state.

Julia C. Bulette was the most famous prostitute from the Silver Rush era of Nevada. She was in all probability one of many popular prostitutes of her day, and was a subtle guest "character" on the television show, *Bonanza* (1959-1973).

Juliette, in 1863, lived and worked from her home on D Street, and was murdered on January 19, 1867. She was found in her room, beaten and strangled. Her killer was later caught, convicted, and hanged. The town mourned and turned out in record numbers for her funeral procession.

The Julia C. Bulette Red Light Museum continued her legacy. There are old photographs depicting some of the business dealings between her and well-known public figures, as well as artifacts, such as an antique vibrator and "lipstick condom case." There are two cabinets filled with contraceptives and early vibrators, rows of naughty shot glasses, whiskey decanters shaped like the state of New Hampshire, a Canadian Mountie human skull, and a shrunken head. A framed photo of a 19th-century Chinese family is incongruously propped next to one of a 1940s actress/pinup queen in a bathing suit, and visitors can also see novelties like bumper stickers and post cards.

A sign hangs up saying, "Julia is remembered for her golden heart and remains Nevada's most celebrated courtesan as people remember the request that 'her faults be buried with her and her virtues live.'"

THE JULIETTE C. RED LIGHT MUSEUM
5 N. C Street, Virginia City, NV 89440
Phone: (775) 847-9394 or (775) 847-9288
Website: http://www.museumsusa.org/museums/info/1165056

Mob Museum. *Photograph courtesy Library of Congress*

THE
MOB MUSEUM

The Mob Museum, the National Museum of Organized Crime and Law Enforcement, is dedicated to the history of organized crime and law enforcement. It was designed by a world-class team known for successful museums, such as the Rock and Roll Hall of Fame in Cleveland and the International Spy Museum in Washington, D.C. This Museum showcases real stories and events of Mob history in a 41,000-square-foot section on three floors in a former historic federal courthouse.

Heading the Board of Directors is President Ellen Knowlton, former FBI Special Agent in Charge, Las Vegas Division, and a twenty-four-year FBI veteran. The goal of the museum is to educate the public by dispelling the legendary "myth of the Mob," and show the role of law enforcement in ending the Mob's reign in

America. Relics displayed include those from Alphonse Capone, Dion O'Bannion, George Moran, Charlie "Lucky" Luciano, Meyer Lansky, Ben Siegel, John Gotti, and Whitey Bulger. The Museum also has artifacts relating to law enforcement's role in helping to eradicate and control the Mob, such as weapons, wiretapping tools, and tactics and crime scene photos. The Mob Museum has state of the art interactive touch screens and visitors can "shoot" a simulated Tommy gun and listen to real FBI surveillance tapes on wiretapping equipment. It even has the real remains of the wall from the infamous Valentine's Day massacre.

If you have an interest in the Mob or the history of the FBI, this is truly a fascinating place.

THE MOB MUSEUM
300 Stewart Avenue, Las Vegas, NV 89101
Phone: (702) 229-2734 Email: info@themobmuseum.org Website: http://themobmuseum.org/

General admission for adults (18+) $18, children (5-17) and students (18-23 w/ID) $12, seniors (65+), military/law enforcement, teachers $14, Nevada residents $10. Hours of Operation: Sundays through Thursdays: 10 a.m. to 7 p.m., Fridays and Saturdays 10 a.m. to 8 p.m.

The Extraterrestrial Highway.
Photograph courtesy Library of Congress

THE EXTRATERRESTRIAL HIGHWAY

People come from the world over to drive along this ninety-eight-mile expanse of Nevada 375. UFO enthusiasts are excited to take this road, hoping to have a close encounter.

There is only one small community along the way, Rachel, with a population of around eighty, so it is a vast and lonely highway. Area 51 is close by, which has been linked to many alien conspiracy cover-ups.

If you watched the movie *Paul*, two British men take a journey to Comic Con and then travel the Extraterrestrial Highway and meet an alien. While this may not be *your* experience, you never know what you may encounter.

ROUTE 275

Route 375 is a state highway in south-central Nevada, stretching from State Route 318 at Crystal Springs northwest to U.S. Route 6 at Warm Springs.

BATTLE MOUNTAIN, NEVADA

Battle Mountain is a small community in a rural and low-populated part of the state. Mining is an important part of the local community, as well as gambling. The story is that it is haunted by a Lady in Blue. According to legend, at some time in the past, a drunk and angry local followed a lady there from out of town into the ladies restroom, and in his drunken anger, killed her. She is said to still haunt the diner.

The Lady in Blue is known to move the light fixtures. She is also said to appear in mirrors, but when you turn around, she is gone. Some claim if you look long enough into the mirror while there, her face will replace yours and then slowly fade away.

It is stories like these that always make me want to travel, searching for the truly eerie along the journey.

BATTLE MOUNTAIN, NEVADA

Battle Mountain is located on Interstate 80 between the town of Winnemucca and Elko.

Little A'Le'Inn Rachel. *Photograph courtesy Library of Congress*

LITTLE A'LE'INN IN RACHEL

If you've watched the *X-Files* television show or the movie *Paul*, then you are familiar with the Little A'Le'Inn. This famous landmark is not only a restaurant, but there are also hotel rooms available, and of course, the famous gift shop.

The rates are extremely reasonable for the rooms, food, and gifts, which makes this a place you really want to go to stretch your dollar along the way.

Little A'Le'Inn in Rachel
HC 61 Box 45, 1 Old Mill Road, Rachel, NV 89001
Phone: (775) 729-2515 Website: http://littlealeinn.com/

DONNA'S DINER

People interested in UFO mythology come from the world over to be near Area 51. With the many movies, television shows, and documentary specials that have been filmed here through the years, you will want to take pictures and feel a part of a very special place run by people who really care about their guests.

Donna's Diner is a nice place to stop off and eat, if you are in the area, a place that is reputed to be haunted. The local legend is that the town drunk followed a tourist into the ladies restroom. In his drunken rage, hc murdered her. Now her ghost haunts the diner.

The diner is no longer in business; however, the building is still there.

Donna's Diner
150 West Front Street, Battle Mountain, NV 89820
Website: www.hauntspot.com/haunt/usa/nevada/donnas-diner.shtml

HARD ROCK CAFÉ LAS VEGAS

Hard Rock Café Las Vegas,
E.R. Vernor with Don "The Vampire" Henrie.
Photograph courtesy of the author

While on a trip to Las Vegas back in 2006 to see an old friend, Don Henrie (yes, Don "the vampire" from SyFy Channel's *Mad Mad House* reality show), he was gracious enough to give me a tour of the city, as it was my first time out there. After a leisurely stroll through the mall, we stopped for a bite to eat at the Hard Rock Café. Not only was the food excellent but I was instantly impressed by the eerie décor. I saw the clothing and props from *Terminator2*, and Gary Oldman's armor from the Coppola film, *Bram Stoker's Dracula*. Well, I handed off the camera to a tourist and Don and I had our picture taken in front of it.

As an interesting side note, the Café started with an Eric Clapton guitar: the beginning of something that nobody even knew was beginning. Back in the Seventies, Clapton ate at this little American diner in London called the Hard Rock Café. The old building used to be a Rolls Royce dealership, and it was run by Isaac Tigrett and Peter Morton, two music lovers. Clapton became friends with the proprietors and asked for a regular table, and asked half kidding if they would put up a brass plaque. One of the young owners said, "Why don't we put up your guitar?" To their surprise, he did just that.

A week later, another guitar arrived—a Gibson Les Paul—and with it was a note from Pete Townshend of The Who that said, "Mine's as good as his. Love, Pete."

Time has passed since then and now there are more than 70,000 items of rock memorabilia on the walls of over 163 Hard Rock Cafés, Hotels and Casinos in 52 countries around the world.

HARD ROCK CAFE LAS VEGAS
3771 S. Las Vegas Boulevard, Las Vegas, NV. 89109
Phone: (702) 733-7625 Email: lasvegas_salescoord@hardrock.com Website: www.hardrockhotel.com

The Hard Rock is open Sunday to Thursday 11 a.m. to 12 a.m., Friday and Saturday 11 a.m. to 1 a.m., and the "Rock Shop"
is opened Sunday through Thursday 9 a.m. to 12 a.m., Fridays and Saturdays from 9 a.m. to 1 a.m.

WHERE TO STAY

★ ★ ★ ★ ★ ★

RON DECAR'S
LAS VEGAS HOTEL

Ron Decar's Las Vegas Hotel is a venue for themed weddings and celebrations with friends and family. The hotel offers honeymoon suites, junior suites, themed rooms, and standard rooms. Themed rooms include Blue Hawaii, Camelot, Cupid, Disco, Egyptian, Gangster, and Goth. Guests who stay in the Gothic room can enjoy a bride and groom coffin bed, blood-red satin sheets, and a coffin-shaped bathtub. Decorations that add to the Gothic feel of the room include a Dracula castle mural, gargoyles, ghosts, tombstones, and some ornate sconces. Couples who want to get married in Las Vegas can book the Gothic Wedding package that includes Dracula or the Grim Reaper as the minister, Gothic lighting and fog, video of the ceremony, and a limousine service to and from the hotel.

RON DECAR'S LAS VEGAS HOTEL
1205 Las Vegas Boulevard South, Las Vegas, NV 89104
Phone: (702) 384-0771 Email: alasvegashotel.com Website: www.alasvegashotel.com

Hard Rock Café Las Vegas Hotel lobby. Photograph courtesy Cheryl Kaopua Senior Public Relations Manager Hard Rock Hotel and Casino

HARD ROCK HOTEL

Hard Rock Café Las Vegas Hotel bar. Photograph courtesy Cheryl Kaopua Senior Public Relations Manager, Hard Rock Hotel and Casino

Hard Rock Hotel in Las Vegas offers Gothic rock rooms in the Casino Tower. The celebrity suites in the Casino Tower have repeating ornamental patterns on the walls that are characteristically Gothic. Other features of the rooms include mirrored walls, wall lamps, wall-sized armoires, a billiard table, and a mini bar. The deep, dark colors of the furniture and decorative pieces add to the Gothic feel. The Casino Tower offers standard guest rooms, executive suites, deluxe suites, celebrity suites, and a penthouse. Large rooms open up to a pool or mountain view of the city.

Hard Rock Hotel. Photograph courtesy Cheryl Kaopua Senior Public Relations Manager, Hard Rock Hotel and Casino

HARD ROCK HOTEL
4455 Paradise Road, Las Vegas, NV 89169
Phone: (702) 693-5000 Email: hardrockhotel.com
Website: www. hardrockhotel.com

NEW HAMPSHIRE

WHERE TO VISIT

THE
PINE HILL CEMETERY

In Hollis, New Hampshire, there lies a cemetery rumored to be a place of paranormal activity. The cemetery land was donated by Benjamin Parker, Jr. in the year 1769. Pine Hill Cemetery sits alongside Nartoff Road and there are over 300 bodies buried there.

One of the stories I discovered is that of Abel Blood, who is buried at the Pine Hill Cemetery. Abel and his wife, Betsy, were murdered and people say that the spirit of Abel Blood roams in attempt to locate his beloved wife. It is said that because of this, it has been nicknamed "Blood Cemetery." However, it is also said that the Hollis locals resent the name, so if you're looking for this location, be sure to refer to it as Pine Hill Cemetery. (Be aware that there are other Blood Cemeteries out there, as well, representing the Blood family throughout the New England area.)

A local warns trespassers that Pine Hill is closed after dark and there are motion detectors that go off if someone enters, alerting the police. Also, Able Blood's stone is no longer there and now rests in an old Church. It was being vandalized, so it was removed.

An interesting fact about this cemetery is that, in the 1800s, an epidemic struck Hollis and the area and so many passed so quickly that a mass burial site (unmarked) was required. There is believed to be between 150-200 people buried there.

A number of individuals go to the Pine Hill Cemetery on ghost hunting trips, many of whom are professional paranormal experts looking to capture images on film and documenting any evidence supporting the hauntings.

PINE HILL CEMETERY
Nartoff Road, Hollis, NH 03049

WHERE TO STAY

★ ★ ★   ★ ★ ★

THE
SPALDING INN

In the scenic area of the White Mountains, The Spalding Inn is owned by the hosts of the show *Ghost Hunters* and The Atlantic Paranormal Society (TAPS), which, as it should be of no surprise, is rumored to be haunted. The Carriage House is still standing and is in full operation, but when people visit, door knobs can be heard moving when no one is anywhere near them.

After buying the inn, TAPS owners Grant Wilson and Jason Hawes heard stories regarding the paranormal activity in the building, such as in the kitchen, where investigators recorded whispers of someone talking, movement in the back area of the room, and shadows.

If you happen to be visiting the inn, you just might run into the *Ghost Hunters* TAPS team.

THE SPALDING INN
199 Mountain View Road, Whitefield, NH 03598
Phone: (603) 837-9300 Email: reservations@thespaldinginn.com
Website: www.thespaldinginn.com

NORTH DAKOTA

WHERE TO EAT

SPACE ALIENS GRILL & BAR

With four North Dakota locations (and two in Minnesota), I would highly recommend taking the trip to this fun chain of prairie restaurants.

The first time I went to Space Aliens, it was in Fargo, and it was an experience I will never forget. Not only was the food extraordinary, the décor was out of this world. Also, being North Dakota, you will never find a friendlier group of servers than at this group of restaurants.

The theme is obviously sci-fi and space oriented. You feel like you are being transported into the deepest recesses of outer space in a flying saucer. There are lots of amazing space memorabilia, such as articles hanging on the walls. While you are waiting for your food, you can walk around and look at all the incredible things they have collected and display.

The ribs and pizza here are excellent. Regardless, there is a wide range or outstanding products on the menu.

SPACE ALIENS GRILL & BAR
NORTH DAKOTA LOCATIONS:
Website: http://spacealiens.com

Bismarck, ND	Fargo, ND	Minot, ND	Grand Forks, ND
1304 E Century Avenue	1840 45th Street SW	1400 31st Avenue SW	3250 32nd Avenue South
Bismark, ND 58503	Fargo, ND 58103	Minot, ND 58701	Grand Forks, ND 58201
Phone: (701) 223-6220	Phone: (701) 281-2033	Phone: (701) 852-7427	Phone: (701) 757-RIBS (7427)

NEW JERSEY

WHERE TO VISIT

THE
BURLINGTON COUNTY PRISON

Located in Mount Holly, New Jersey, this rumored haunted prison attracts both tourists and professional ghost hunters alike. It opened its doors in 1811 and includes a house on the property that was designed for the warden, connected to the prison by a tunnel. In 1965, the prison closed due to overcrowding, as it housed more than double the individuals it was created to incarcerate.

In 1999, renovations began at the prison, to turn it into a museum, but whispers began that ghosts were making their presences known, causing many of the workers to abandon the job site, never to return.

The owners called in a team of paranormal experts who thoroughly investigated the prison. They concluded that this *was* a haunted place with a number of angry spirits, and said they heard strange noises in the area where past inmates took their showers when the Burlington Prison was open and operating.

THE BURLINGTON COUNTY PRISON
Grant Street and High Street, Holly NJ 08060
Phone: (609) 265-5476 or (609) 518-7667
Website: http://prisonmuseum.net/

Visitors are allowed during open business hours, Thursday through Saturday 10 a.m. to 4 p.m., and on Sunday, from 12 p.m. to 4 p.m. Adults: $4, Seniors and Students: $2, Children under five years of age can visit for free.

THE SOUTHERN MANSION

Industrialist George Allen constructed the large Southern Mansion in New Jersey as a summer getaway in 1863. It is rumored to be haunted.

One of the rooms in the home seems to have a paranormal presence. It is believed that a death occurred in this room, and people who enter claim that they feel the emotions and tension of this presence.

However, not all of the reported spirits are sad or angry. When many have visited the Mansion, they hear laughter and, at times, a beautiful woman is observed dancing, believed to be George Allen's niece.

THE SOUTHERN MANSION
720 Washington Street
Cape May, NJ 08204
Phone: (800) 381-3888
Website: www.southernmansion.com

WEST MILFORD, CLINTON ROAD

THE INFAMOUS HAUNTED ROAD IN NEW JERSEY—CLINTON ROAD: "AMERICA'S MOST TERRIFYING THOROUGHFARE."

—The Travel Channel, *Most Terrifying Places in America*

One road in New Jersey that has gained the reputation of being haunted is a ten-mile stretch in the township of West Milford known as Clinton Road. Many of these experiences have been featured in books, such as *Convergence: When the Living Clash with the Dead*. Locals say that it is a place where cults come to worship Satan and there have been sightings of unidentified creatures, like the "wolf-like" "hell hounds" talked about for well over a century.

WEST MILFORD, CLINTON ROAD

Clinton Road is located in West Milford, Passaic County, New Jersey. It heads in a north-south direction, beginning at Route 23 near Newfoundland and spanning 10 miles until it reaches Upper Greenwood Lake.

NEW MEXICO

WHERE TO VISIT

INTERNATIONAL UFO MUSEUM & RESEARCH CENTER

The International UFO Museum and Research Center was founded by the people who took part in the Roswell incident. Located in Roswell, New Mexico, the legend of the Roswell UFO crash of 1947 lives on. This is the perfect place to indulge your curiosity! The museum has outgrown two locations since it first opened in 1991. Activities around the UFO incident include trade shows, alien costume contests, a gift shop, and visits from Hollywood celebrities.

INTERNATIONAL UFO MUSEUM AND RESEARCH CENTER
114 N. Main Street, Roswell, NM 88203-4706
Phone: (575) 625-9495 Website: http://www.roswellufomuseum.com/

ALBUQUERQUE, OLD TOWN

Old Town is a historical section in Albuquerque, New Mexico, and it is said that the entire town is haunted, with over a dozen ghosts in various buildings and alleyways. The Maria Teresa Restaurant has reported that ghosts like to play the piano for the staff late at night. Both the Church Street Cafe and Bottger Mansion Bed and Breakfast have spirits, as well. Tour the city to hear and visit the many other strange tales.

OLD TOWN

Visitors' Information Center, Plaza Don Louis
303 Romero Street NW, Albuquerque, NM 87104
Website: http://albuquerqueoldtown.com/

Open 7 days a week. Operating hours: May 1st to October 31st: 10 a.m. to 6 p.m. and November 1st to April 30th: 10 a.m. to 5 p.m. Old Town is made up of individually operated businesses. Each location determines their own days and hours of operation. Most businesses are open Monday through Saturday from 10 a.m. to 8 p.m. and on Sundays from 11 a.m. to 7 p.m. Most restaurants will seat patrons until 9 p.m. The **San Felipe Church Ghost Tours** are offered every night at 8 p.m. for a $20 fee. Tours are also available on Friday and Saturday at 10 p.m., with private tours are offered for 6 or more people.

NEW YORK

WHERE TO VISIT

★ ★ ★ ★ ★ ★

SING SING PRISON MUSEUM

In Ossining, New York, lies a museum near the Sing Sing Prison. You will see authentic confiscated weaponry, where the curator demonstrates the proper use of shanks and "eye gouging" techniques in prison fights. You even get to see a replica electric chair on display, hand-crafted in flawless detail. The real chair executed 614 inmates. Two mock cells are available where visitors can have their photos taken, and even former inmates are known to visit with their families.

SING SING PRISON MUSEUM
95 Broadway
Ossining, NY 10562-4101
Phone: (914) 941-3189
Website: www.crimemuseum.org/library/
imprisonment/singsing.html

THE CITY HALL SUBWAY STATION

Under the busy streets of New York City rests the abandoned and yet pristine City Hall Subway Station, constructed over 100 years ago, as part of New York's earliest underground transport network. The site of the 1900 groundbreaking, this station was designed to be the showpiece of the new subway. It was shut down in 1945, largely due to the nearby Brooklyn Bridge, and lay untouched until it was opened as a public exhibition on the station's centennial. The original southern terminal of the Interborough Rapid Transit subway is unusually elegant in architectural style; it is unique. The curved platform is about 400 feet long, and features Guastavino arches and skylights, colored glass tile work, and brass chandeliers.

THE CITY HALL SUBWAY STATION
Website: http://nycsubway.org/wiki/
Abandoned_and_Disused_Stations

The New York Transit Museum occasionally grants tours of this station, but these have been suspended at the time of this printing due to perceived security risks of City Hall.

KINGS PARK PSYCHIATRIC CENTER

In 1885, the Kings County Farm housed the poor and mentally ill. The farm colony originally opened with fifty-five patients. As buildings were added, the patients increased as well. The asylum's overcrowding lead to protests by the public and medical staff, which lead to the state taking over in 1895. By the 1900s, the patient population had grown to well over 2,000 with a staff of 400, and more than a hundred permanent buildings, including a bakery, laundromat, amusement hall, bandstand, library, furniture repair shop, and nursing school. In 1954, Kings Park Psychiatric Center (KPPC) housed over 9,000 patients. The Kirkbride Building had to be modernized, as running water, fire escapes, and other new technologies were worked into building codes, making the basements a nightmarish maze of pipes and wires squeezing into the spaces of the old design. The central administration portion was still used, however, until around 2001, when the property went up for sale and was eventually sold to a developer.

New changes in treatment and the medical plan changing in America to "decentralize" psychiatric patients into community facilities or outpatient treatment later reduced the need for the hospital. All the patients were eventually moved out of the Kirkbride sometime around the mid 1970s, and the wards have since fallen into major disrepair. By the 1980s, KPPC was a shell of its former self, with many buildings being abandoned as it was forced to cut costs, and by 1996, the Center closed and its remaining patients were transferred to Pilgrim State.

A story from one of the urban explorers claimed they encountered a girl after they'd entered a room, the only exit door being locked. They say that the girl told them that they didn't belong there and she screamed at them to leave the place. They tried the door and yelled back to her that the door was locked. Once more, the girl screamed that they didn't belong and to leave, and with this, the door unlocked without the assistance of the explorers. As they left the room, they looked back and the girl had vanished.

The developers began restoration with plans to preserve the entire Kirkbride. However, in June 2007, the male wing caught fire, caused by lightning, and destroyed much of this section of the building; the larger of the two wings is now a burned-out shell. The exterior walls have gaping holes that span two floors and the roof is missing in most parts. Restoration efforts have since halted.

The 1995 movie, *Eyes Beyond Seeing*, was filmed in KPPC's Building 136/137 (old medical/surgical unit) shortly after the building was closed down. The film also contains exterior shots of the famous Building 93. In 2009, another movie about the legend of Mary Hatchet was brought to the screen in *Blood Night: The Legend of Mary Hatchet*, an urban legend in the form of a ghost story.

Although the main hospital is closed off and patrolled by the police, the Kings Park Heritage Museum offers guided tours by appointment only, where one can see replicas.

KINGS PARK PSYCHIATRIC CENTER
RJO Building, 99 Old Dock Road, Kings Park, NY 11754
Phone: (631) 269-3305 Email: Info@KingsParkMuseum.Com
Website: http://www.kingsparkli.com/2008-Info/Heritage.htm

Genesee County Poor Farm, Rolling Hills Asylum. *Photograph courtesy Tim Shaw*

ROLLING HILLS ASYLUM

ocated somewhere between Buffalo and Rochester sits an enormous brick building on a hill in East Bethany, New York. Opened on January 1, 1827, Rolling Hills Asylum was originally known as The Genesee County Poor Farm. Created by the county to house those eligible for assistance—which meant the poor, the town drunks, and lunatics. Mixed in with the undesirables were the blind, handicapped, orphans, and widows. In the 1990s, the building was renovated into a set of shops and an antiques mall. When the property's vendors and shoppers began to notice strange occurrences, a paranormal group was called in to investigate the building. After that, the Rolling Hills reputation grew and it soon became a popular spot for ghost hunters who report voices, doors frozen shut, screams at night, and what is known as shadow people.

Rolling Hills Case Manager Suzie Yencer relates her frightening experience, saying:

It was September 2007. While working a public hunt, we had a gentleman with us who was filming a documentary about the building. He wanted to try an experiment in one of the rooms. The room he chose was in the basement, popularly known as The Christmas Room. The experiment he wanted to try was to sit in the room with no lights or equipment on. The only light we would use was a pink glow stick in the middle of a circle of people. We also placed a small ball and a toddler size rocking horse in the circle. The gentleman conducting the experiment requested that only I talk and try to make contact with the spirits. The more I talked, the more strange occurrences began to happen. The glow stick started to move back and forth, and the rocking horse began to slowly rock. A few of the guests in the room, including myself, saw a hand and arm come out of nowhere and reach for the ball in the circle and then just vanish....

ROLLING HILLS ASYLUM
11001 Bethany Center Road
East Bethany, NY 14054 Website: http://rollinghillsasylum.vpweb.com/

Tours: 8 hours for private hunt, maximum 10 people, by appointment only.

FEATURED NEW YORK LOCATION!

OBSCURA ANTIQUES & ODDITIES

Obscura Antiques & Oddities is the basis for a documentary/reality television show on the Discovery Science Channel called *Oddities* that premiered on November 4, 2010. I found myself catching wind of the show while my friend, Marilyn Mansfield (the maker of scary dolls) was on it and began seeing it as often as possible. *Oddities* is a half-hour program that follows the operation of a Manhattan shop in the East Village that trades in antiques and other rarities related to circuses, sideshows, taxidermy, and natural history. The show focuses on the day-to-day operation of Obscura Antiques & Oddities, and stars co-owners Mike Zohn and Evan Michelson, along with buyer Ryan Matthew, with appearances by other very unique customers and people they buy from.

The store came into being a long time ago, with both owners having diverse pasts and interests in odd things. Mike Zohn discovered antiques one day while learning how to drive; he got lost and came across an antique store housed in an old barn. Mike's curiosity for odd knickknacks was sparked, and he continued buying odds and ends he found fascinating, some of which he sold at a profit in order to supplement his salary as a photo researcher. In not very long at all, Mike found himself with so much "stuff," he realized he either had to seek help for hoarding or open a store. His partner at Obscura Antiques & Oddities is fellow collector and museum aficionado Evan Michelson, who stops to smell the roses away from the busy life at the shop by

resting at cemeteries. Evan was part of a former Gothic/industrial/post-punk band called Killer Weasel in the 80s, and has always had a passion for the dark and bizarre. She has been interested in anatomical/medical antiques and artistic depictions of the extremes of human experience where, in her words, "art melds with pain and ecstasy," as well as a love of the macabre esthetics of grief. Evan also collects Victorian hair-work and has the nickname of "Morticia Addams."

Ryan Matthew is a buyer for Obscura Antiques & Oddities, a collector of horror-movie props since he was a child, and now collects things he is interested in for the shop: Victorian taxidermy, skulls, and skeletons (as he has an interest in the medical field, exploring human and animal structure, and in taxidermy). He started by cleaning and trying to re-articulate the skeletons of animals that his dog killed and brought back to him. That, as well as a love of Victorian taxidermy made him a perfect fit in a shop fit for The Addams Family.

In the words of Mike Zohn, "We deal in the odd and unusual; a lot of the people we deal with are as odd as the objects themselves." Celebrities often appear on the show, including Jonathan Davis of the band Korn, director Lloyd Kaufman, musician Voltaire, and Church of Satan member Marilyn Mansfield, among countless other people who were just as unique and amazing as the store itself.

Oddities. Photograph courtesy Discovery Science Channel

The shop houses many items and changes frequently in what it has to offer, including a mini coffin complete with skeleton, a mummified cat, a Rhesus monkey skull, grotesque multi-headed animals in jars of formaldehyde, vintage straitjackets, taxidermied lizards, and any number of items you might find in a cabinet of curiosities from the Old West to the Victorian Era. The hosts of the show spend a lot of time traveling to locations in search of treasures to purchase, or visiting eccentric collectors who hire them to locate a special item.

If you ever find yourself in Manhattan, please stop by and check it out for yourself!

OBSCURA ANTIQUES & ODDITIES

207 Avenue A (Just below 13th Street In Manhattan) New York, New York 10009-3474
Phone: (212) 505-9251 Email: info@obscuraantiques.com Website: http://www.obscuraantiques.com

Hours: Monday to Saturday noon to 8 p.m., Sunday noon to 7 p.m.

Oddities. *Photograph courtesy Discovery Science Channel*

Oddities. *Photograph courtesy Discovery Science Channel*

Oddities owner Mike. *Photograph courtesy Discovery Science Channel*

Oddities owner Evan. *Photograph courtesy Discovery Science Channel*

AMITTYVILLE HOUSE

The media madness and later marketing frenzy following *The Amityville Horror* book and movie began back in late 1974. A local man named Ronald DeFeo shot his entire family in the early morning hours at his house in Amityville, Long Island, New York. In court, it was discovered that DeFeo massacred his family to collect $200,000 in insurance money, resulting in a closed case with a confession of murder—but this tale of suburban angst was given new life when the Lutz family moved into the DeFeo house.

A bestselling book in 1977, and a hit movie two years later, made this Long Island house popular despite the fact that investigative reporters revealed the Amityville horror story as a well-crafted hoax between Ronald DeFeo, George and Kathy Lutz (the original owners of the house) and William Weber (DeFeo's defense attorney).

The house's current owner, Brian Wilson denies any sightings of anything supernatural, and this feeling is shared by Ric Osuna, an associate producer for a documentary titled *The Amityville Horror: 25 Years Later.* Previous owners James and Barbara Cromarty, who lived a decade in the house, said, "Nothing weird ever happened, except for people coming by because of the book and the movie."

THE AMITYVILLE HORROR HOUSE

The 112 Ocean Avenue address has now has been changed to 108 Ocean Avenue.
The house is .3 of a mile down on the left, opposite South Ireland Street.

THE
HAUNTINGS OF SLEEPY HOLLOW

Sleepy Hollow dates all the way back to the early 1600s, to when Europeans discovered the area and settled there, but it was not until the Dutch arrived that it was given its name, "Slapershaven." In translation, it means "Sleeper's Haven." It wasn't until the year 1996 that the town's name was officially renamed to that we know it by today.

Washington Irving's tale *The Legend of Sleepy Hollow* was a fictional piece; however, few know that it was based on facts, old local legends, and people who are actually a part of this ghost town's haunted history, like the Headless Horseman's character. A Hessian soldier was captured during the American Revolutionary War in Patriot's Park between the cities of Sleepy Hollow and Tarrytown. He was immediately executed by way of beheading. This apparition is often said to linger throughout the area, and Irving took this legend of the soldier for his tale.

Irving also took ownership of "Sunnyside," a name for a home in Sleepy Hollow in 1835. This small, ordinary cottage sits on the bank of the Hudson, where many claim to have seen Irving himself as a restless spirit.

You can visit the grave of Irving, as well as Andrew Carnegie, William Rockefeller, and Walter Chrysler at the Sleepy Hollow Cemetery. Visitors claim they hear weeping when no one else is present late at night. Find out exactly how spooky Sleepy Hollow is for yourself!

SLEEPY HOLLOW CEMETERY
540 N. Broadway, Sleepy Hollow, NY 10591 Phone: (914) 631-0081
Website: www.sleepyhollowcemetery.org

Hours are Monday through Friday: 8:30 a.m. to 4:30 p.m.

Fort Ticonderoga.
Photograph courtesy public domain

"IT'S A VERY HAUNTED PLACE."

— Trisha Melton, *Fort Ticonderoga employee*

FORT TICONDEROGA

During the American Revolutionary War, in May 1775, the British were defeated; Fort Ticonderoga was abandoned by the British after the British Army, under General John Burgoyne, surrendered at Saratoga. Early on in the nineteenth century, William Ferris Pell, who built a summer home on the property, opened it as a hotel for the tourists who were interested in visiting what was left of the old fort. The descendants of William Pell began restoring Fort Ticonderoga during 1908, and in 1909, it was opened to the public.

While there are many haunted places in New York, Fort Ticonderoga is one of the most notable for its paranormal activity. Numerous reports have been made by the employees and visitors of what seems to be paranormal activity on the grounds, and there are thousands of soldiers buried there that might make these claims believable. People report hearing sounds, such as footsteps, hoof beats, and voices.

The Fort conducts reenactments, twice per year, of the historical battles that took place there, yet at other times of the year, when the building has been closed, there have been claims by staff members that they have spotted people dressed in eighteenth century-style military clothing. TAPS investigated the fort for their television show *Ghost Hunters* and say they managed to catch several EVPs and witnessed "an unexplainable illumination of a room, seen by two teams at the same time who were located in two different areas." Jason Hawes of TAPS stated during the reveal to staff member Christopher Fox: "I firmly believe that you have paranormal activity going on here."

If you are interested in seeking out haunted places in New York, the fort offers ghost tours at night, by reservation only, during the summer months.

FORT TICONDEROGA GHOST TOURS
100 Fort Road, Ticonderoga, NY 12883
Phone: (518) 585-2821 Website: www.fort-ticonderoga.org

WHERE TO STAY

SHANLEY HOTEL

In the city of Napanoch in the state of New York, the Shanley has attracted many paranormal investigators.

In the year of 1845, the hotel was originally named "Hungerford's Hotel" and was constructed by Thomas Rich. The hotel continued to change ownership numerous times over a period of three decades. In 1906, James Louis Shanley purchased the establishment.

Over the years, the haunted Shanley Hotel has faced many tragedies, as various murders occurred at the location. Because of this, visitors claim there are several hauntings. Many of the hauntings seem to be that of James Shanley, as well as a woman that can be heard mourning. Some visitors say they have seen a woman in a beautiful Victorian-style dress. The third floor is particularly scary.

If you want to experience the haunted Shanley Hotel for yourself, make your reservations!

SHANLEY HOTEL
56 Main Street, Napanoch, NY 12458
Phone: (845) 210-4267 Website: http://www.shanleyhotel.com

Otesaga Resort Hotel.
Photograph courtesy Otesaga Resort Hotel, Cooperstown, New York

Otesaga Resort Hotel Ballroom.
Photograph courtesy Otesaga Resort Hotel, Cooperstown, New York.

THE
OTESAGA RESORT HOTEL

The Otesaga Resort Hotel was built in the early 1900s on Otesaga Lake's southern shore in a small village called Cooperstown within the State of New York. Not only is the Otesaga a member of the Historic Hotels of America program, but it also has the reputation of being one of the most haunted hotels in New York.

Staff and guests who have stayed at the Otesaga Hotel have reported many unusual experiences, include children running and furniture moving on floors where there are no occupants.

Ghost hunters from TAPS investigated the Otesaga Hotel for an episode of their television show (aired August 25, 2010). The fifth floor hallway and rooms 585 and 307 were investigated. The investigators advised that they saw and heard many of the same things visitors and staff members have reported. The team assured everyone that there was "likely nothing to fear from these permanent guests, as they are basically just revisiting the place they may have once enjoyed when they were alive."

If you have an interest in staying at a haunted New York hotel, the Otesaga is a fantastic choice.

THE OTESAGA RESORT HOTEL
60 Lake Street Cooperstown, NY 13326
Phone: (800) 348-6222 Website: www.otesaga.com

Otesaga Resort Hotel. *Photograph courtesy Otesaga Resort Hotel, Cooperstown, New York.*

NORTH CAROLINA

★ ★ ★ WHERE TO VISIT ★ ★ ★

THE MORDECAI HOUSE

Located in Raleigh, North Carolina, the Mordecai House was constructed in the 1780s by Joel Lane, named after Lane's granddaughter, Margaret Mordecai, who eventually passed away there. Many visitors say they have heard the sound of the piano playing, only to discover the appearance of a female apparition at the instrument. Others visiting the house have reported sighting spirits of men who served in the Civil War lingering on. When the last of the family passed away, the home was turned into a historic landmark and tours were given to preserve the history of the plantation. Tour guides and tourists alike claim that when guides named people who have lived at the house, their pictures fell off the walls!

The Mordecai House in Raleigh is a must see.

MORDECAI HOUSE
1 Mimosa Street, Raleigh, NC 27604 Phone: 919-857-4364
Website: www.visitraleigh.com/.../Mordecai-House-Ghost-Tours/21107

THE
USS NORTH CAROLINA

The historic battleship, the USS *North Carolina*, located in Wilmington, North Carolina, is open to the public as a museum at Eagle's Island. The ship was originally commissioned on April 9, 1941 and had almost 2,000 men as crew in her early days. Under the command of Olaf M. Hustvedt, the *North Carolina* was created to protect aircraft carriers during several wars and was highly decorated, with fifteen different battle stars for her successful endeavors during varied wars served. Despite all of the wars, the ship survived with only ten casualties.

Rumor has it that a ghost lingers behind on its final home, wandering the passageways aboard the massive vessel.

The USS *North Carolina* is open every day of the year, including all holidays, and serves as a memorial.

USS NORTH CAROLINA
North Carolina Eagles Island, P.O. Box 480, Wilmington, NC 28402-0480
Phone: (910) 251-5797 Website: www.battleshipnc.com

The tour is self-guided and is well-marked so that you can tour at your own pace. We recommend allowing at least two hours for the tour, but for the true enthusiast, you can spend much more than that. Price of admission: Adults, 12 and over $12.00; Seniors 65 and over $10.00.

OHIO

WHERE TO VISIT

CHESTNUT GROVE CEMETERY

Chestnut Grove Cemetery in Ashtabula, Ohio, is the resting place of those who died in the great train wreck of 1876. Caretakers of the graves and visitors say the place is haunted.

It was December 1876 when a heavy snowstorm covered the railroad tracks and the bridge collapsed into the creek below from the sheer weight of the train and its content. Many individuals died of hypothermia, while others succumbed to the fires ignited by various oil-burning lamps.

Bodies were placed in a single grave in the Chestnut Grove Cemetery, and the company who made the bridge, Charles Collins and Amasa Stone, was put to an inquiry investigation by the local government who held them responsible for the deaths. Collins gave his account to the jury, and on his walk home, shot himself in the head. Stone, some two weeks later, killed himself as well. Collins and Stone were buried in the Chestnut Grove Cemetery near the victims of the accident, and it is believed that the spirits of Collins and Stone are now walking the grounds, looking out towards the bridge.

CHESTNUT GROVE CEMETERY
831 Dranesville Road, Herndon, VA 20170
Phone: (703) 435-3480 Email: mike.moore@herndon-va.gov
Website: http://www.chestnutgrovecemetery.com/

MANSFIELD PRISON

Cited by the Travel Channel as one of the "101 Things to Do Before You Die," the Ohio Penitentiary (also known as the Mansfield Prison) is indeed a place to see. Constructed in 1834, it was actually the second Ohio Penitentiary. By April 1955, it housed an all-time record of over 5,000 inmates. There are over 200 numbered grave markers laid out on the property. Most were victims of disease, influenza, and tuberculosis, but some were deaths from violence and suicide. Even the keepers of the inmates were not safe from death's icy grip—in 1950, in the warden's living quarters, the warden's wife, while removing a jewelry box from a closet shelf, dislodged a pistol's hiding place. It struck the floor and fired a fatal shot. Later, in the same decade, the warden suffered a heart attack and died in his office.

I remember seeing the film inspired by Stephen King's short story, "Rita Hayworth and the Shawshank Redemption," for one of my criminal justice classes. The most rented/purchased video of 1995, it featured Tim Robbins as the innocent man convicted and Morgan Freeman, the man who becomes his friend. It was used for various backdrops throughout the prison scenes in the *Shawshank* film, as well as in the 1989 film *Tango and Cash*, starring Sylvester Stallone and Kurt Russell. Contrary to popular belief, the *Beautiful People* video by shock-rocker Marilyn Manson was not shot at Mansfield Prison, but *was* the location of a photo shoot for a Marilyn Manson magazine spread.

Since the prison's closure, there have been rumors that people see the spirits of tortured inmates who died there, and if history is any indication, I have no doubt that if spirits exist anywhere, it would be here!

MANSFIELD PRISON
100 Reformatory Road, Mansfield, OH 44905
Email: info@mrps.org Phone: (419) 522-2644 Website: www.mrps.com

There are three tours to pick from on Sundays, every 15 minutes in a rotating manner. The prison website describes the tours as follows:

EAST CELL BLOCK TOUR
Travel the length of the East Cell Block, the world's largest freestanding steel cell block. On this tour, you will pay a visit to the Catholic Chapel above the Central Guard Room. Gain insight into the living quarters as you venture through multiple floors. This tour involves extensive steep stair-climbing and other hazards, including uneven surfaces, lead-based paint, and other dangers. It is not recommended for pregnant women.

HOLLYWOOD TOUR
See the office of the prison warden from *Shawshank Redemption*, the Parole Board Room, and Andy Dufresne's escape tunnel. Hazard a trip into the sinister "hole." View the 1886 West Cell Block, used as a Russian prison in *Air Force One*. This tour also involves extensive stair-climbing. Tickets are $9 for adults and $7 for seniors, military, and ages 7-17. Haunted X Enterprises, LLC, conducts ghost investigation tours, with an admission price of $65 per person, which includes access to the building from 8 p.m. until 5 a.m. and a late dinner of pizza and drink. Overnight paranormal investigation is for ages 21 and over.

WEST TOWER TOUR
Experience the view from the Guard Tower after winding up the spiral staircase. From this perspective, you will see the cemetery where inmates were buried with only their assigned number on the grave. This tour also stops at the Big Dig, where you can observe the underground tunnel system. There is extensive stair-climbing on this tour. Taking pictures from the wall or Guard Tower portion of this tour is not permitted.

MARY STOCKUM'S GRAVE

Stockum Cemetery, a small family cemetery, long-ago abandoned, is located south of OH-541, outside Coshocton, Ohio, in Linton Township, Coshocton County. All of the gravestones have been broken and vandalized.

Many people claim to have experienced problems there with their vehicles, thought to be caused by the angry spirit of Mary Stockum, who haunts the cemetery and the woods around it. Mary, never married and having no children, was beheaded during a robbery at her home and found by her milkman. Her body was placed in a grave at the cemetery without her head, which wasn't found until thirty days later in a water well.

STOCKUM CEMETERY

Finding the Stockum Cemetery is a little challenging, but it can be done: Take OH-541 east out of Coshocton. Once you pass TR-123 on the right, look for the "Caution—Haul Road" sign on the right. Turn onto the next road: Gravel Haul Road. You'll eventually come to an intersection. Turn left. After turning left, the road will soon come to a fork. Veer to the left, onto the dirt road to the cemetery.

FRANKLIN CASTLE

Franklin Castle has the distinction of being a historic house, located at in Cleveland, Ohio. A spectacular "haunted house," complete with a tower, turrets, balconies, stone outcroppings, gargoyles, wrought-iron fixtures and fences, this imposing, Gothic-style home was built in 1860 for Hannes Tiedemann, an immigrant from Germany who became a banker. Three mysterious deaths of babies occurred in the house between 1865 and 1895. Hannes Tiedemann was overbearing and cruel, yet was never formally accused during his lifetime of the deaths, let alone tried or convicted. Nonetheless, it is rumored he also killed his daughter and a servant.

Presently, Franklin Castle is owned by a businesswoman who wishes to turn it into a bed and breakfast, but a fire in 1999 greatly slowed the process.

FRANKLIN CASTLE
4308 Franklin Boulevard, Cleveland, OH 44113
Phone: (216) 631-CLUB Email: info@franklincastleclub.com
Website: www.deadohio.com/franklincastle.htm

OKLAHOMA

WHERE TO STAY

THE SKIRVIN HOTEL

In the year 1910, a wealthy oil man named W.B Skirvin dreamed of owning the most popular and "finest" hotel establishment in the Southwest, and to be among the first to provide air conditioning and cold running water for his guests. By 1911, The Skirvin Hotel was open for travelers. It was created with two towers, ten stories high—very tall for its day—with 224 beautifully designed, elaborate rooms.

Although it was well used, after World War Two it suffered a major loss of income and changed hands after its original owner's death.

It is believed to be haunted by the spirit of a woman who had an affair with W.B Skirvin in the thirties, and became pregnant. The young lady committed suicide by jumping to her death from the top floor while she held her baby.

The hotel is on the National Registry, and finally reopened for business in 2007.

THE SKIRVIN HOTEL
One Park Avenue, Oklahoma City, OK 73102
Phone: (405) 272-3040 Website: www.skirvinhilton.com

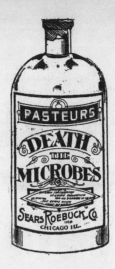

THE
STONE LION INN
BED & BREAKFAST

Constructed in the year 1907, this amazing Victorian mansion once served as a funeral home. Originally, the structure was built to serve as a home for Mr. Houghton and his family. However, soon after, one of his daughters developed "whooping cough," and died because the doctors issued the wrong type of medication.

The mid-1980s saw the old place receive a new owner, Becky Luker, who claims the renovations woke the spirits of the house. She says a great many doors seemed to open randomly, and also shut by themselves. Her son would put away his toys every night, and in the morning, they would be scattered around again. Guests tell stories of several haunting experiences, such as the appearance of children playing in the rooms and jumping on the beds, even when none were staying at the inn.

Now a stately inn, The Stone Lion has been thoroughly restored, recapturing the innovative style and appearance that it had in the early days. This beautiful bed and breakfast holds a murder mystery dinner, starting with a trip to the local cemetery; then the guests solve a murderous crime as part of their stay.

THE STONE LION INN BED & BREAKFAST
1016 West Warner, Guthrie, OK 73044
Phone: (405) 282-0012 Website: www.stonelioninn.com

OREGON

★ ★ ★ WHERE TO VISIT ★ ★ ★

THE
OREGON VORTEX

I'm a sucker for a roadside attraction. I love driving along and stopping at the largest ball of yarn or any attraction that builds itself up as a mystery. For those of you who, like me, enjoy such places, the Oregon Vortex is for you.

According to locals, a building was erected on the site, in 1904, by a mining company to serve as an office. It is said that miners would come to the office to have their gold weighed, but were confused when the scale's readings were largely off. In 1910, the building slid off its foundation and rested at an odd angle, at which it remains to this day.

At this fun attraction, odd angles give an illusion of objects rolling uphill. The attraction is famous for its height change illusion, where the height of two people can change due to a distorted background.

The attraction also has a great gift shop with mementos that cannot be found anywhere else.

Whether you are traveling with the family, a group of friends, or even alone, make sure you stop at this curious roadside attraction that has been a staple of Oregon tourism for decades.

THE OREGON VORTEX
4303 Sardine Creek Left Fork Road, Gold Hill, OR 97525-9732
Phone: (541) 855-1543 Email:mystery@oregonvortex.com Website: oregonvortex.com

FLAVEL HOUSE MUSEUM

Besides allegedly being haunted, the Flavel House Museum is a beautiful estate and one of the best preserved examples of Queen Anne architecture in the Pacific Northwest. If you want to accurately see the elegance of the Victorian Era, look no further. Also, for movie geeks, the house appeared in the classic film *The Goonies*.

The estate was once the home of Captain George Flavel, one of the most influential citizens of the area. His home was completed in 1886, but he only lived there for seven years, passing away in 1893. The house stayed in the family until George's great-granddaughter gave the property to the city. Over the years, there had been talk of tearing the building down, but citizens organized to save the great estate, and finally, the county transferred the title to the historical society in 1995.

There are many reports of hauntings in this house-turned-museum. There have been reports of strange music coming from the music room, once the entertainment room of the home. Many people report feeling a presence in the Captain's library where the family spent most of their time.

The second floor is where the family members had their own separate rooms. There have been many reports of paranormal occurrences in the hallway. Apparently, apparitions have been seen thought to be one of the daughters. In Mary Flavel's room, there are claims of a sudden floral scent that comes out of nowhere, and moves around the room. It is almost as if Mary is walking about the area, but no one can see her.

There have been accounts in the Captain's room by both staff and visitors of the ghost. Some report to feel light-headed or nauseated when they are in this room.

Whether you are a fan of *The Goonies* movie or a fan of the supernatural, the Flavel House Museum is a must see.

FLAVEL HOUSE MUSEUM
441 8th Street, Astoria, OR 97103-4620
Phone: (503) 325-2203
Website: http://www.cumtux.org/default.
asp?pageid=35&deptid=1

Shanghai Tunnels. Photograph Michael Jones owner of Shanghai Tunnel Tour

SHANGHAI TUNNELS

If you want to take an interesting tour of a wicked piece of Oregon history, the Shanghai Tunnels is the place to go.

The tunnels, and the phrase "to have been Shanghaied," comes from the kidnappings that occurred within these tunnels. This was a wicked, yet clever, practice where men were kidnapped and sold to boat captains who then forced them to work aboard their ships for no pay. Portland had taverns with trap doors where barkeep would drop victims into cells with barred doors. The victims would be kept forcibly in these cells until the appropriate ship was set to sail. This was the Portland Underground, or Shanghai Tunnels as it became known when it was seized by authorities, this name due to the fact that most of the captors were sold to crews bound for Shanghai, China.

The Portland Underground was made up of basements in buildings that were interconnected by way of brick or stone archways beneath the streets. This network of tunnels was used to transport women for prostitution, as well.

SHANGHAI TUNNELS
120 NW Third Avenue, Portland, OR 97209
Phone: (503) 622-4798
Email: shanghaitunnels@onemain.com
Website: www.shanghaitunnels.info/

Tours available: Monday to Sunday 4 p.m. to 2:30 a.m.

★ ★ ★ ★ ★ ★

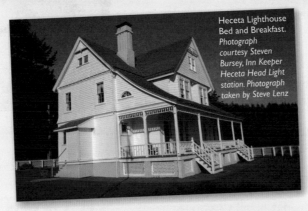

Heceta Lighthouse Bed and Breakfast. *Photograph courtesy Steven Bursey, Inn Keeper Heceta Head Light station. Photograph taken by Steve Lenz*

HECETA LIGHTHOUSE BED & BREAKFAST

I love lighthouses, so I can't think of anything better than staying overnight at one. For anyone who feels the same, there is no finer place to go than the Heceta Lighthouse Bed and Breakfast. Not only are you staying at a lighthouse, you are staying at one of the most photographed lighthouses in the United States. While you don't actually have to stay here to enjoy it—there are tours given of the lighthouse itself—wouldn't you like to have the whole experience, which may include a ghostly encounter?

On the grounds, called Devil's Elbow, is a long abandoned grave of a baby girl, who was thought to be the daughter of one of the early lightkeepers of the facility. While you may not find the grave, it is thought to be the focal point of the famous Grey Lady that is said to haunt the lighthouse.

Every keeper who has worked here since the 1950s has reported strange things. There have been screams heard in the night, objects that go missing, closed cupboards have been found open, and lost tools and such showing up later in strange places.

Aside from any ghost that you may encounter, you will certainly enjoy the beauty and majesty of this amazing location.

HECETA LIGHTHOUSE BED AND BREAKFAST
92072 Highway 101 South, Yachats, OR 97498
Phone: (866) 547-3696 Email: keepers@hecetalighthouse.com Website: hecetalighthouse.com

Tours are given daily, March through October, from 11 a.m. to 5 p.m. The lighthouse observation area is open year round during park hours. To arrange a tour beyond the regular tour season, please call 1-800-551-6949. For more information, visit Oregon State Parks. The Heceta Head Lighthouse Gift Shop is located in the old generator room between the Lighthouse and Keeper's House.

Heceta Lighthouse Bed and Breakfast. *Photograph courtesy Steven Bursey, Inn Keeper Heceta Head Light station. Photograph taken by Steve Lenz*

WHERE TO EAT

★ ★ ★ ★ ★ ★

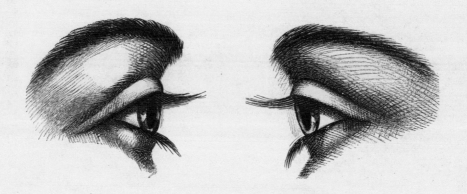

YE OLDE CASTLE RESTAURANT

Ye Olde Castle Restaurant is a restaurant and antique shop that goes back to the 1800s, when it was a private residence.

There have been sightings of a ghostly woman in a blue dress for quite some time. It is said by witnesses that she will stare at you, and when you attempt to make eye contact back, she will disappear. They also say that even as she vanishes, you can feel her standing there. When the restaurant is being repainted or repaired, she makes most of her appearances. According to many ghost hunters, this is common since the ghosts are not happy with people making changes.

YE OLDE CASTLE RESTAURANT
186 West Monroe Street, Burns, OR 97720 Phone: (541) 573-6601

PENNSYLVANIA

WHERE TO VISIT

NEMACOLIN CASTLE

The name for this castle is derived from an individual who was Native American and helped the white settlers in their endeavors in moving across the country to the West. However, the actual structure was built by the Bowman family. While there are several rooms and passages within the castle that are quite interesting, what is even more fascinating is that the castle is said to be haunted with several lingering spirits.

Visitors have taken photographs that seem to indicate a ghostly presence caught on film. While many fear the spirits at the castle, the locals and employees of the mansion have stated that there is no reason to be frightened, as it appears that these are friendly ghosts. There are believed to be approximately ten different ghosts, though no one understands exactly where they originated from. Many believe that the castle may serve as a portal to the spiritual world from the physical one; however, accounts regarding the hauntings indicate that the same spirits seem to haunt the location over and over again.

The hauntings at this castle are so strong that now the area hosts ghost tours allowing individuals to try and catch a glimpse of the friendly spirits that linger in the castle and on the grounds. If you visit, it is not unusual to smell cologne and perfume that cannot be explained or footsteps walking near you where there is no one else present.

NEMACOLIN CASTLE
100 Front Street, Brownsville, PA 15417-1933
Phone: 724-785-6882 Website: www.nemacolincastle.org

Castle fee schedule of all tours (including ghost tours) $8 adults/$4 for 12 & under.
History tours every Friday, Saturday, and Sunday: noon through 5 p.m. all three days. Summer Festival: July 26, 27, 28.

Hall of Presidents in Gettysburg. A strange and creepy mannequin kept in the basement. It is said that something ghostly turns this figure's head at night from time to time — when no one is in the building. Photograph courtesy of Dinah Roseberry.

GETTYSBURG BATTLEFIELDS

When ghost hunters think of places haunted in Gettysburg, Pennsylvania, the Gettysburg Battlefields of the Civil War are the places to visit first. In that single event in America's history, lasting for three days of brutal fighting, almost 50,000 individuals met an untimely and traumatic deaths in 1863. Even though it has been centuries later, people still report hearing mournful cries of the ghosts of these Civil War battlefields.

Mark Nesbitt, expert on all things haunted in Gettysburg, is an award-winning author and paranormal investigator who has been on television documentaries and radio programs across America, has a tour company called Ghosts of Gettysburg, and is available to travelers seeking to experience the paranormal side of historic Gettysburg.

GHOSTS OF GETTYSBURG
271 Baltimore Street, Gettysburg, PA 17325
Phone: (717) 337-0445 Website: ghostsofgettysburg.com

CASHTOWN INN

In 1797, the Cashtown Inn was built and opened for business. Located on the famous Route 30, it was very popular, so much so that the Confederate Army, commanded by the General Robert E. Lee, ordered his troops to station there until he decided his next course of action, which ultimately was the infamous "Battle of Gettysburg." The Cashtown Inn became a triage impromptu hospital.

Business eventually slowed to a near standstill by the year 1948, because the town allowed a bypass highway to be constructed, thus diverting the flow of traffic that had been the lifeblood of the hotel for decades. Carol Buckley, and Charles, her husband, bought the building in 1987.

As with The Stone Lion Inn, once they began the restoration process, many paranormal events began. Visitors have reported that rocking chairs move on their own, along with reports of knocking sounds in their rooms. Employees and visitors have heard other unexplained sounds when no one else was around. Visit the hotel and see for yourself!

CASHTOWN INN
1325 Old Route 30, Cashtown, PA 17310
Phone: (717) 334-9722 Website: www.cashtowninn.com

The restaurant is open Tuesday through Saturday.

Lunch: 11:30 a.m. to 2 p.m.; Dinner: 5 p.m.

THE
WEDGEWOOD INN

This quaint and cozy 1870 Wedgwood House is a functioning and spacious Victorian tourist spot, a colonial restored inn located in New Hope, Pennsylvania. It is open all year long and spans over two acres of landscaped grounds, not far from the bustling village of New Hope and the walking bridge to Lambertville. This historic bed and breakfast inn combines such modern amenities as in-room two-person Jacuzzis, fireplaces, and Wi-Fi, with Victorian splendor and romantic queen and king lace-canopied beds, tall ceilings, lofty windows, pine floors, and more.

This bed and breakfast was a site for the Underground Railroad and has hidden passageways that were also used by abolitionists. Psychics and the owners, Nadine and Carl Glassman, claim the inn is haunted, but by very friendly spirits. Come stay here and find out for yourself!

WEDGWOOD INN
111 W. Bridge Street, New Hope, PA 18938-1401
Phone: (215) 862-2570 Website: www.wedgwoodinn.com

FARNSWORTH
BED & BREAKFAST

Located near the battlefields, the Farnsworth Bed and Breakfast was constructed in 1810. The house was named in memory of Elon John Farnsworth, Brigadier General, who was promoted to this rank on the same day as his ill fated charge, when he and sixty-five of his men perished.

During the first day of the Battle of Gettysburg, the Confederate soldiers took over the house and placed sharpshooters in the attic when the house had come under heavy fire. There are still over 100 bullet marks seen in the south side of the building. The attic and basement, as well as many guest rooms are said to be haunted, including the Sweney Room, McFarland Room, Sara Black Room, and Jennie Wade Room. There are said to be at least fourteen ghosts that haunt the estate; many are thought to be those spirits of former soldiers.

In 1972 a family purchased the home and restored it. Now the establishment provides lodging, historic and ghost tours. This inn has been featured on A&E, Discovery, Syfy, and the Travel Channel who calls it "One of the most haunted inns in America."

FARNSWORTH BED AND BREAKFAST
401 Baltimore Street, Gettysburg, PA 17325
Phone: (717) 334-8838
Website: www.farnsworthhouseinn.com/

FEATURED
PENNSYLVANIA LOCATION!

THE MÜTTER MUSEUM

Mutter Museum Hyrtl skull collection. *Photograph courtesy Eric Miller, Museum Director photo taken by George Widman*

AUTHOR NOTE:
I JUST KEPT ON GOING WHEN WRITING THIS ONE! THERE WAS JUST SO MUCH! IT WAS MY FIRST REAL LOCATION TO GO TO MYSELF AND IT INSPIRED THE BOOK!

—E.R. Vernor

I had the pleasure, a few years back, to tour The College of Physicians of Philadelphia and the Mütter Museum and it was one of the moments that began this very book. Eric Miller, the Lecture and Communications Coordinator for The College of Physicians of Philadelphia, was very helpful in providing me with information on the College itself and on the Museum.

The nation's oldest medical society, The College of Physicians was founded in 1787 by a group of physicians, including Dr. Benjamin Rush, one of the signers of our nation's Declaration of Independence. The college was created for physicians to better serve the public, as a place to gather scientific and medical knowledge from America and abroad. They sought to use this information to educate the public and encourage high standards of professional practice.

Now, over 200 years later, The College of Physicians continues their legacy as a non-profit educational entity and, along with The Mütter Museum, America's finest medical museum, home to over 20,000 objects, including medical instruments, specimens, illustrations and memorabilia of outstanding physicians and scientists, is now open to educate the public on the history of the museum and showcase its treasures.

The collection began as a donation from Dr. Thomas Dent Mütter, who was determined to improve and reform medical education. At the time Mütter was a student at University of Pennsylvania's medical school, students were not allowed to work with patients or assist with medical surgical procedures. His disappointment with American teaching techniques drove him to Paris to receive hands-on training. Upon his return to the States, Mütter assembled the collection and offered it to the College with a $30,000 endowment. The donation stipulated that the College had to hire a curator, maintain and expand the collection, fund annual lectures, and erect a brick building to house the collection.

The College has held true its promise to Dr. Mütter; today the museum enjoys a steadily rising reputation with attendees exceeding 100,000. Enjoying international popularity, the museum has been featured in a documentary on the Discovery Channel. The College's Museum features a wide collection of many bizarre yet fascinating displays: one of the most recent additions is the brain of Albert Einstein. Others that are just as noteworthy are:

Soap Lady

Fiber-optics now light up the Plexiglas display case of what is famously known as the Soap Lady. For more than 130 years, the contorted face of a bony woman, has been forever frozen in mid scream, her bony hands pressed against her sides. Ellenbogen was exhumed back in 1875 in a kind of mummified state. Her flesh had been transformed through a rare chemical reaction into a soapy substance called adipocere.

Some time back, after the museum closed, radiographers and forensics technicians used high-tech portable X-ray equipment. Using digital X-rays as guides, samples of tissue were removed from her liver and a kidney. As best as researchers could find, she probably suffered from yellow fever in 1792.

Dr. Joseph Hyrtl's Human Skull Collection

Prominent Viennese anatomist Joseph Hyrtl had amassed an enormous collection of human skulls from around the world, including that of Wolfgang Amadeus Mozart, which he inherited upon the death of his brother, Jacob, in 1868. The skulls have a wide geographic range, from Amsterdam, Albania, Armenia, Austria, Australia, Bohemia, Bulgaria, Czechoslovakia, Crete, Croatia, Egypt, Finland, Galicia, Greece, Hong Kong, Hungary, Italy, Lebanon, Lithuania, Malta, Moldavia, Prussia, Romania, Russia, Serbia, Switzerland, Thailand, and Transylvania to name most. Ranging from age 8 to 80, but most of the people making up Hyrtl collection seem to have died in their early 20s and represent several causes of death, including death by "dagger trust" to the tight rope walker who died of a broken neck.

In 1874, a committee representing the Mütter Museum of the College of Physicians of Philadelphia completed their negotiations with Joseph Hyrtl to buy 139 skulls from Central and Eastern Europe for their own collection.

The image here is of one of their most popular exhibits, the Hyrtl Skull, in the Mütter Museum, provided courtesy Eric Miller, the Lecture & Communications Coordinator.

Gretchen Worden was the most famous museum staff curatorial assistant in 1975, then later the director in 1988. Worden was a frequent guest on the Late Show with David Letterman, "displaying a mischievous glee as she frightened him with human hairballs and wicked-looking Victorian surgical tools, only to disarm him with her antic laugh" and appeared in numerous PBS, BBC documentaries to educate people on the marvels of the museum.

Plaster cast and Conjoined Liver of "Siamese twins" Chang and Eng

Chang and Eng were identical twins that lived and died in Mount Airy, North Carolina. The conjoined twin brothers were born on May 11, 1811, in Thailand, with a Chinese heritage (as they were born from a Thai Chinese father). Chang and Eng, known as the "Chinese Twins," were joined at the sternum by a small piece of cartilage and fused livers, each independently complete. Nineteenth-century medicine did not have the means to separate them.

In 1829, a British merchant named Robert Hunter found them and exhibited the twins as a curiosity on a world tour, but later Chang and Eng successfully went into business for themselves. In 1839, while visiting Wilkesboro, North Carolina, the twins became citizens and purchased a plantation, renaming themselves Chang and Eng Bunker. On April 13, 1843, they married two sisters: Chang to Adelaide Yates and Eng to Sarah Anne Yates.

After the Civil War, they again resorted to public exhibitions, with much less success. The twins died on the same day in January 1874, of pneumonia—Chang first, in his sleep. Eng woke up and called for his wife, who summoned a doctor in order to perform an emergency separation, but Eng refused to be separated from his dead brother, and died three hours later.

The fused liver of the Bunker brothers was preserved and is currently on display at the Mütter Museum, as is the life-sized sculpture of them.

The Mütter Museum The College of Physicians of Philadelphia
19 South 22nd Street, Philadelphia, PA 19103 Email: info@collegeofphysicians.org
Phone: (215) 563-3737 Website: www.collphyphil.org/site/mutter_museum.html

Business office hours: Monday to Friday, 9 a.m. to 5 p.m., Museum hours:
Open daily, 10 a.m. to 5 p.m., Historical Medical Library: By appointment, Tuesday, Wednesday, and Thursday, 10 a.m. to 4 p.m.

★ ★ ★ WHERE TO STAY ★ ★ ★

EASTERN STATE PENITENTIARY

A few years ago, I visited Philadelphia, and while there, I passed the infamous Eastern State Penn, as it is called, whose foreboding size and history is the stuff of documentaries, not to mention a ghost hunter's delight. When Eastern State Penitentiary opened in 1829, it quickly grew into what Charles Dickens described of the inmates' conditions as appalling, as if they were "buried alive…" No doubt the psychological torture the inmates suffered gave Dickens some of his inspiration for the demeanor of the convict in the book *Great Expectations*, especially the beginning meet up with Pip, the lead character of the classic tale.

To this day, visitors from around the world marveled at the Gothic architecture. The incredibly high arched cathedral, with thousands of skylights, add to the imposing feel that God is watching the visitors as if they were the condemned, being ushered along inside, waiting in purgatory before a visit to Hell.

Cited as one of America's most historic prisons, the official website claims that "Eastern State Penitentiary was once the most famous and expensive prison in the world, but stands today in ruin, a haunting world of crumbling cellblocks and empty guard towers." This was the world's first true penitentiary, "designed to inspire penitence, or true regret, in the hearts of convicts." Its vaulted Gothic architecture housed many of America's most notorious criminals, including the notorious Al Capone.

Rumored to be haunted and the subject of multiple ghost hunter shows, such as *Paranormal State*, the *Travel Channel's Ghost Adventures* and *Most Haunted Live*, as well as Syfy's *Ghost Hunters*, MTV's *FEAR*, and more, it has drawn thousands of people out of curiosity, from researchers and historians to ghost enthusiasts. Many books have been written about it, such as *Philadelphia Haunts: Eastern State Penitentiary, Fort Mifflin, & Other Ghostly Sites* (by Katharine Sarro), *Ghostly Tales from America's Jails, Ghost Stories of Pennsylvania,* and *Philadelphia Ghost Stories.*

People have reported ghostly apparitions, footsteps, tapping, and voices, and visitors and investigators have been touched, pushed, and worse.

EASTERN STATE PENITENTIARY
2027 Fairmount Avenue, Philadelphia, PA 19130
Phone: (215) 236-3300 Website: www.easternstate.org

The prison fees to tour are $8 to $12 depending on age, 10 a.m. to 5 p.m. (last entry 4 p.m.),
every day, twelve months a year, except for Thanksgiving, Christmas Eve, Christmas Day,
and New Year's Day. Don't forget to visit the gift shop! The prison holds a truly scary haunted attraction on Halloween.

SATAN'S SEAT

S atan's Seat is an underwater town, also known as Livermore, that, in the 1800s had a witch living among the people. Tragically, she was put to death— they burned her alive. As she died, she placed a curse on the town and a flood covered the area, causing the deaths of the people who lived there. To this day, there are still corpses in the town. When the water is low enough, you can see the tops of chimneys and houses.

The "Livermore Cemetery" sign is the same one used in the original black and white zombie film by George Romero's *Night of the Living Dead*. For more information check out the Livermore's Westmoreland Historical Association.

SATAN'S SEAT
Livermore Road, Perry County, Livermore, PA 17045

Located 40 miles east of Pittsburgh, take I-376 east to High 22/East William Penn;
turn left at Livermore Road and continue straight.

CITY TAVERN RESTAURANT

O riginally constructed in 1772, this landmark is a good place to stop for a mix of relaxation, food, and of course, chilling ghost stories! The present structure is a reconstruction of the original, which was destroyed in a fire in 1854. The fire not only claimed the City Tavern, but a young bride and several of her friends upstairs, while the groom's party was downstairs waiting elsewhere. It appears that during the rush of preparations, no one in the bridal party noticed that a candle had tipped over, or possibly an oil lamp, which burst into flames. The drapes caught fire, as did the rug near the bridal party, which caught the train of the bride's dress. In no time at all, the entire room was engulfed in flames.

The groom and his attendants attempted to save the bride and her ladies, but were largely unsuccessful. The bride and many of her attendants perished, and the City Tavern had to be demolished. What a sad ending to what was to have been the happiest day of a young bride's life!

The City Tavern was rebuilt and reopened in 1976, and continues to host events. People have held wedding parties there and have made claims that in the photos they take, there is the image of an unknown woman wearing what looks like a bridal gown. Some patrons have claimed to have seen the apparition of the phantom bride in the halls and rooms of the tavern.

THE CITY TAVERN
138 South 2nd Street at Walnut Street, Philadelphia, PA 19106
Phone: (215) 413-1443 Website: http://www.citytavern.com/

Lunch is served from 11:30 a.m. daily; dinner is served from 4 p.m.
Monday through Saturday, from 3 p.m. Sundays.

RHODE ISLAND

WHERE TO VISIT

★ ★ ★ ★ ★ ★

SPRAGUE MANSION

William Sprague built the Sprague Mansion in 1790. Amasa Sprague added to the home and transformed it from a farmhouse into the mansion it is today. He made his fortune in the textile business in New England. In 1843, he left his home on a business trip—a trip he never really made, as his body was found on the grounds beaten to death. John Gordon was found guilty of his death and was hanged for the murder, although it was later discovered that Gordon most likely did not commit the crime.

Many have claimed that there are spirits living in the Sprague Mansion, and this goes as far back as the year of 1925. It is said that the spirit of Amasa is still haunting the house, seen both on the staircase and in the wine cellar. People since have added more contemporary ghost encounters at the Sprague Mansion, and have claimed to have seen a ghostly female, with one visitor saying that he has actually been touched by the spirit. Some say that their bedding was pulled off when they were sleeping, and in the doll room, the lights would flicker on and off. TAPS, the group behind the popular show *Ghost Hunters,* have even conducted an investigation at the establishment.

BELCOURT CASTLE IN NEWPORT

This Rhode Island castle is a beautifully designed sixty-room chateau, huge and elegant, created by architect Richard Hunt. Oliver Belmont was the first owner and, in 1908, he died, leaving Alva, his beloved wife, the estate.

The current owner runs ghost and historic tours, as well as events, such as weddings.

People say that the original collection of armor at the establishment that was collected and owned by the ever-popular Oliver has been seen moving with no one inside it. A mirror in the castle is also said to be haunted—if you look into the glass, there is no reflection looking back!

SPRAGUE MANSION
1351 Cranston Street, Cranston, Rhode Island 02920
Phone: (401) 944-9226
Website: cranstonhistoricalsociety.org/
The Mansion hosts wedding, receptions, and other similar events.

BELCOURT CASTLE
657 Bellevue Avenue
Newport, RI 02840
Phone: (401) 846-0669
Website: www.belcourtcastle.com

SOUTH CAROLINA

WHERE TO VISIT

THE
OLD CITY JAIL

Constructed in 1738, The Old City Jail is located in Charleston, South Carolina. It originated as a place where slaves served and the homeless could get medical care. In 1790, this jail housed notorious criminal offenders, as well as those needing a mental asylum. Today, it is considered to be a haunted jail; many claimed they have seen the ghost of a former slave of the property wandering throughout the halls of the building.

A tour is offered with the local ghost tour company for $17.50 and lasts for approximately forty-five minutes.

OLD CITY JAIL
21 Magazine and 17 Franklin Streets
Charleston, SC 29401

BULLDOG TOURS, INC.
40 North Market Street, Charleston, SC 29401
Phone: (843) 722-8687 Website: bulldogtours.com

WHERE TO EAT

★ ★ ★   ★ ★ ★

POOGAN'S PORCH RESTAURANT

Poogan's Porch is one of the oldest restaurants in Charleston. It has been recognized by *Martha Stewart Living, Wine Spectator,* and The Travel Channel. They are known for their fresh approach to Low Country cuisine.

The establishment was originally built as a stately Victorian home in 1888, and in 1976, it was turned into a restaurant. The establishment is named for a dog who stayed behind when the former owners left. He is said to have claimed the porch for himself. Poogan the dog was well known in the neighborhood, going from porch to porch for attention. When the establishment first opened, the dog was the official greeter, and even after his death, he has not been forgotten.

The restaurant has been a favorite haunt of politicians, celebrities, tourists, and locals. The food is known all around the region, and they have a state of the art 1,500 bottle wine cellar, the kind of spirits we can all enjoy.

The restaurant was named as one of the most haunted places in America by the Travel Channel in 2003. It is said to be haunted by Zoe St. Armand, a former resident of the house who died there in 1954. Guests of the Mills House Hotel, next to the restaurant, have at times reported noticing a lady in black waving to them from across a second-story window. She is said to like to play tricks and is known to move things around. At times, she appears angry and will push things off a table.

Regardless, if you enjoy both a good haunt and good food, go no further than this fine establishment.

POOGAN'S PORCH RESTAURANT
72 Queen Street, Charleston, SC 29401-2220
Phone: (843) 577-2337 Website: www.poogansporch.com

★ ★ ★   ★ ★ ★

THE
BATTERY CARRIAGE HOUSE

The Battery Carriage House is the kind of bed and breakfast I love. They advertise their alleged hauntings, rather than hide it. A place like this will appeal to anyone who reads this book.

The bed and breakfast is known as Charleston's most haunted inn and reportedly home to several ghosts. The owners claim to have not seen any of them, but say the guests and employees have had many odd occurrences.

The first report listed goes to 1992, about a ghost with a headless torso. It is said the spirit may be a young man whose family owned the place at one time. Supposedly, the man had jumped off the roof, committing suicide for no good reason. The headless torso is said to most likely be a soldier from the Civil War era, since the inn was an active artillery installation during the siege of Charleston, and all the homes in the area were damaged and abandoned during this time.

Rooms 3, 8, and 10 are listed as the most haunted ones. Room 8 appears to have experiences with the headless torso. Room 10 has the most experiences with the gentleman ghost. Visit the website of the establishment to read about some of the inn's posts from past guests. Then make a reservation here, especially in one of the haunted rooms.

THE BATTERY CARRIAGE HOUSE
20 S. Battery, Charleston, SC 29401
Phone: (843) 727-3100 Website: www.batterycarriagehouse.com

SOUTH DAKOTA

WHERE TO STAY

THE
HOTEL ALEX JOHNSON

In 1927, a man named Alex Johnson founded this establishment. He was the Vice President of the Chicago and Northwestern Railroad and was an admirer of the Sioux Indians. When he designed the hotel, he added Native elements, as well as German, to create his masterpiece.

The hotel has plenty of ghost stories; the most famous is one of the "Lady in White" who haunts the 8th floor of the hotel, especially room 812. She stayed at the hotel quite often, but on one fateful day, she jumped from a window on the 8th floor to her death. People who knew her believed that she did not jump and that it was murder, due to her wealth.

Visitors to the hotel investigating the specter say that she wants others to know that her death was not a suicide. Guests who stay in her old room claim they find that the window is often wide open without reason. Visitors also claim to hear the faint sounds of ghostly piano music, and the faint sobs of a female with no one on the floor, other then the person hearing the ghost.

THE HOTEL ALEX JOHNSON
523 Sixth Street, Rapid City, SD 57701
Phone: (800) 888-ALEX (2539) Website: www.alexjohnson.com

THE
BULLOCK HOTEL

No visit to South Dakota is complete without a visit to Deadwood. I went a few years back with my mother to trace our family heritage and was informed that we were related to Wild Bill Hickok on our American side (the other side is French).

The namesake of the Bullock Hotel, Seth Bullock, arrived here in 1876. He opened a successful hardware store on the current site of the hotel. Seth had been sheriff in Lewis and Clark County, Montana, before arriving in Deadwood and took over after the death of Wild Bill.

In time, Bullock and his partner, Sol Star, decided to build a fine hotel over the store. When the place was complete, it had a restaurant that could seat 100 people, a large lobby with red velvet carpeting, brass chandeliers, oak trim, and a grand piano. There were 63 rooms with oak dressers and brass beds. It was one of the most sought after places to stay during that time.

Mr. Bullock is still reputed to haunt his old hotel. He has been seen in many areas of the establishment from the restaurant to the basement. It is alleged that he wants to make sure the staff is working hard, since many paranormal activities take place when staff members stand idle.

Guests are purported to have heard their names called out by a male voice when no one is around or they have been tapped on the shoulder when there was no one behind them.

It seems, according to dozens of reports, Seth Bullock continues to play host at his beloved hotel. All manner of strange occurrences have happened at the historic location, including feelings of a strong paranormal presence inside several of the rooms and in the hallways of the second and third floors, as well as in Bully's Restaurant and in Seth's Cellar. The sound of footsteps when no one is around is also common.

The hotel was also the subject of the television show *Unsolved Mysteries*. It offers a ghost tour for those of you interested in the paranormal, and if you are reading this book, I know that includes you.

While there, be sure to dine at Bully's. You will certainly enjoy your meal, as many others before you have. Give them a call, make reservations, and have a grand adventure in Deadwood.

BULLOCK HOTEL
633 Main Street, Deadwood, SD 57732
Phone: (605) 578-1745 or (800) 336-1876
Website: www.historicbullock.com/

TENNESSEE

WHERE TO VISIT

★ ★ ★   ★ ★ ★

THE
BODY FARM

I first heard about this by a worker at the Body Farm when I was taking a course on forensic criminology doing my criminal justice degree. Right next to The University of Tennessee at Knoxville's Medical Center is an acre of land known as The Body Farm, which belongs to the university's Forensic Anthropology Center. Established in the year 1981 by Dr. William Bass, head of the Anthropology Department, in order to study postmortem changes that occur in a human body, it has been of great importance for forensic scientists, CSI workers, and Law Enforcement. Fifty or more bodies are usually in various state of decay around the site. Some are submerged in water, while others are in the trunks of cars; still others are left exposed in the open. The processes that take place during decomposition of the corpses are photographed and reports handwritten by researchers to help them understand the varying aspects for things like expert witness testimony for court cases. This has been so important, a judge who was dying requested his body be taken to the location, the guest speaker told the class!

THE BODY FARM
FORENSIC ANTHROPOLOGY CENTER,
DEPARTMENT OF ANTHROPOLOGY
250 South Stadium Hall, Knoxville, TN 37996-0760
Phone: (865) 974-4408 Website: http://fac.utk.edu/

Visitors should call to arrange for a visit.

BELL WITCH CAVE

The Bell Witch is a ghost story in American folklore. The legend of the Bell Witch centers on alleged events experienced by the Bell family of Adams, Tennessee. According to the legend, the haunting began in 1817.

John Bell and family moved to Roberson County in 1804, and in the summer of 1817, they started hearing knocking sounds on the doors and outer walls of the house at night. Later, sounds were being heard inside the house, such as that of a rat gnawing on things when there were no rodents in the house, chains being dragged through the house, and a woman making weird noises. They asked who it was, and the family claimed a voice stated that it was the witch of a woman named Kate Batts, an eccentric neighbor of John Bell's, who in life had sued him for cheating her in a land deal, so the people began to call it "Kate" the "Bell's Witch." Betsy Bell, the family's younger daughter was violently attacked, her face slapped by an invisible force. In 1820, John Bell died, and people claimed the witch poisoned him.

In 1819, U.S. President Andrew Jackson decided to observe the phenomena for himself. As he was traveling through the Bell property, his group encountered an invisible presence that stopped his wagon. When Jackson acknowledged that the witch was responsible, the wagon was able to proceed unhindered. One of the men in Jackson's entourage declared himself to be a witch tamer who intended to kill the spirit, but then he began screaming and contorting. Jackson and his entourage left the following day. He is quoted as later saying, "I'd rather fight the entire British Army than to deal with the Bell Witch."

Filmmakers today are said to have used The Bell Witch as the basis for the 2006 film called *An American Haunting* and *The Blair Witch Project* (1999). Not too far away from the original farm, the Bell Witch Cave is privately owned and tours are given during the summer and the month of October.

BELL WITCH CAVE
430 Keysburg Road, Adams, TN 37010
Phone: (615) 696-3055 Website: www.bellwitchcave.com/

The Ryman Auditorium.
*Photograph courtesy
Library of Congress*

THE
RYMAN AUDITORIUM

One of the most famous haunted places in Nashville is one of its legendary tourist attractions, the Ryman Auditorium—most well known for its hosting of the Grand Ole Opry. The structure is officially recognized as a "National Historic Landmark" and is listed in the "National Register of Historic Places." The Ryman Auditorium was originally constructed in the late 1800s by Thomas Green Ryman, for people attending religious "tent revivals" that were popular during that era. Originally built in 1892, it was given the name "Union Gospel Tabernacle" until the year of 1904 when Thomas Ryan died. Then it was renamed the "Ryman Auditorium" in honor of its founder. In 1943, the auditorium was picked as the new location for the Grand Ole Opry,.

Famous for not only music, there is also "the Grand Ole Opry Curse,"with over thirty-five individuals connected to untimely and tragic deaths, such as Patsy Cline and Jim Reeves, the murder of "Stringbean Akeman," and the car crash that took the life of Ira Louvin.

There are several different spirits that are said to haunt the Ryman Auditorium; even the employees at the Ryman claim to have seen the ghost of Hank Williams, Sr. Another frequently reported sighting is that of the original owner, Thomas Ryman. Many speculate that Mr. Ryman is showing his disapproval of some of the performances by creating disturbances during those particular shows.

THE RYMAN AUDITORIUM
116 5th Avenue N., Nashville, TN 37219
Phone: (615) 889-3060 Website: www.ryman.com

WHERE TO STAY

★ ★ ★   ★ ★ ★

THE
READ HOUSE HOTEL

Located on Broad Street, in the downtown area of Chattanooga, Tennessee, and opened during the Civil War under the name of Crutchfield House, this hotel was often referred to as the "Radisson Read House Hotel" (but now known as the Sheraton Read House Hotel) and has been the resting place of Andrew Johnson and Ronald Reagan, among others.

Back in 1863, this structure was a hospital for the Union Army, but in 1867, a fire burned it down. Dr. John T. Read decided to rebuild it as a hotel in the same spot.

On this location, The Read Hotel saw a great deal of murders, suicides, and natural causes of death. As a result, guests and workers have said the place was haunted, especially room 311. Guests there claim to have seen shadowy images in the mirrors and fleeting images of spirits moving in the room. A woman died in this room and some of the tales around it say she was a murdered prostitute.

THE SHERATON READ HOUSE HOTEL CHATTANOOGA
827 Broad Street, Chattanooga, TN 37402
Phone: (423) 266-4121 Website: www.sheratonreadhouse.com

TEXAS

WHERE TO VISIT

★ ★ ★   ★ ★ ★

DRISKILL HOTEL

Opened for business in 1886 by Jesse Lincoln Driskill, this hotel was a popular location for politicians, celebrities, and more, who have conducted business within the walls of this spectacular hotel.

Several people who worked at the Driskill around the time of Jesse Lincoln Driskill's death claimed to continue to feel his presence afterward. Another spirit said to haunt the establishment is a lady who committed suicide on the fourth floor of the hotel. Many individuals claim to have observed what appears to be a spirit of a female out of the corner of their eye while on this floor, but when they look to see who is standing there, no one is there at all. There is a story that in the year of 1887, the young girl of a popular senator of the time met her fate while chasing a ball along the "Grand" staircase in the hotel, where she fell and died; yet, a week after her death, people say they saw her playing at the hotel with her ball.

DRISKILL HOTEL
604 Brazos, Austin, TX 78701
Phone: (512) 439-1234 Website: http://www.driskillhotel.com/

NATIONAL MUSEUM OF FUNERAL HISTORY

Located in Houston, The National Museum of Funeral History respectfully sets out to "preserve the rich heritage of the funeral industry." It is the country's largest collection of funeral service artifacts, features, and renowned exhibits on one of man's oldest cultural customs. "Any day above ground is a good one," is the saying here. Come discover the mourning rituals of ancient civilizations, see up-close the authentic items used in the funerals of U.S. presidents and popes, and explore the rich heritage of the industry that cares for the dead. A casket factory exhibit, information on the art of embalming, and various hearses round out the dignified display, as well as a funeral school located on the premises.

NATIONAL MUSEUM OF FUNERAL HISTORY
415 Barren Springs Drive, Houston, TX 77090-5918
Phone: (281) 876-3063 Website: http://nmfh.org/

Hours: Monday to Friday 10 a.m. until 4 p.m., Saturday 10 a.m. until 5 p.m., Sunday 12 p.m. until 5 p.m.
Admission: adults $10, seniors/veterans $9, children $7 Children under three are free.

MUSEUM OF THE WEIRD

The Museum of the Weird boasts a collection to rival The Ripley's Museum! It is located on 6th Street in downtown Austin, in the same building as Lucky Lizard Curios & Gifts. These type of museums were originally known as dime museums; the first one ever to exist was "The American Museum," opened in 1841 by none other than P. T. Barnum, catering to a poor, common man, and offering items to delight and trick the viewer into what was real and what was a "humbug," as P. T. Barnum called a hoax or fake display.

This museum is the home to a motley assortment of bizarre curios, including shrunken heads, the Fiji Mermaid and a Bigfoot display. Visitors are impressed by the employees. They rocked and were super friendly! I have you classified as "a weird"—you will feel at home.

MUSEUM OF THE WEIRD
412 East 6th Street, Austin, TX 78701
Phone: (512) 476-5493
Website: http://www.museumoftheweird.com/

Museum Admission: $5 Adults, $3 Kids under 8. Hours are 11 a.m. to 11 p.m., 7 days a week (open 'til midnight on Fridays and Saturdays). The museum is closed for certain holidays, so please call ahead to confirm. It is free to enter the gift shop, and entrance to the museum is only $5 for adults, $3 for kids under 8. Open daily 11 a.m. to 11 p.m. They offer senior citizen, student, and military discounts for $4. You get FREE admission with a $20 purchase.

USS *LEXINGTON* IN CORPUS CHRISTI

One of the most haunted ships in the United States is the USS *Lexington*, located in Corpus Christi, Texas. Since being commissioned in 1943, this massive vessel has been nicknamed *The Blue Ghost* and also *Lady Lex*. It now serves as a museum for those who enjoy learning about its history. In days past, the USS *Lexington* served in twenty-one battles out of twenty-four in the Second World War. *The Blue Ghost* is worthy of its nickname due to its color and the spirits that are said to linger onboard, most of which come from a time when a Japanese fighter plane crashed into the ship.

In certain areas of the *Lexington*, such as in the Switch Room, people say they have very uncomfortable feelings and have even become sick, this including Donna from the TAPS *Ghost Hunters* television show. The engine room is another hot spot in the museum for ghostly activity. In battle, when it was hit by the Japanese plane, many servicemen lost their lives. Now tourists say that they hear screams coming from the room.

USS LEXINGTON MUSEUM ON THE BAY
2914 N. Shoreline Boulevard
P.O. Box 23076, Corpus Christi, TX 78403
Phone: (800) LADY-LEX   (361) 888-4873
Website: www.uslexington.com

RIPLEY'S MUSEUM & ODDITORIUM

At this Ripley's Odditorium, you will find all sorts of family fun. Adults can enjoy a shooting range with unusual targets and the whole family will delight in the "Louis Tussaud's Palace of Wax," where you will experience 200 figures of movie stars and historical figures, all filled with "fantasy and fear," as described by the museum. Inside you will be delighted by Hollywood's most famous stars, past and present, and you'll relive unforgettable moments from classic movie stars, horrors films, and the Hall of Presidents.

Ripley's Museum also has another attraction called the Enchanted Mirror Maze, with over 2,000 square feet containing 100 back-to-back mirrors, with LED lighting and digital sound. As you enter the mysterious maze, the room is filled with brilliant green lasers coming from the walls. As you navigate through the web of lasers, you will go over and under beams as quickly as possible to reach the final laser beam, where you will press a stop button, completing your challenge and determining your time and score. Kids especially will enjoy the maze and "Laser Race," which is a timed event. The object is to navigate the maze without breaking a beam. However, if you do break the beam, that's okay. You are simply penalized by time being added to your score.

If you don't make it to the Dallas Ripley's Museum, and are instead visiting San Antonio, be sure to visit the one in Alamo City.

RIPLEY'S MUSEUM AND ODDITORIUM
601 E. Palace Parkway, Grand Prairie, Texas 75050
Phone: (972) 263-2391
Website: http://www.ripleys.com/grandprairie/

Open weekends from 10 a.m. to 6 p.m. Tickets: single attraction, $16.99 adult ticket, $8.99 child (age 4-12). 4-way combo (Ripley's, Wax, Mirror Maze, and Laser Race) $29.99 adult ticket, $19.99 Child (age 4-12).

THE
F.S. WHITE SANITARIUM

Located at the corner of California and Olen Roads, The F.S. White Sanitarium opened in 1926 under the direction of Frank S. White, previously a superintendent at the state asylum in Austin. He was an advocate for providing a non-institutionalized lifestyle for his patients, to diminish the effects of the asylum itself on their mental health.

Abandoned in 1939 after it was damaged from severe flooding, the sanitarium remained a local spot for vagrants and teens until 2002, when Gilbert Rios, a 70-year-old retiree, purchased the building for $15,000. The low cost was a result of the horrific stories about the place, which made it so no other investors wanted it.

Locals tell stories of ghosts inside, still playing cards. "Everyone has heard stories and they range from seeing a woman with long, white hair roaming the place to screams and yells being reported all the way at the other end of the street," says a local resident.

Gilbert Rios himself wasn't a believer in the supernatural; he wanted to fix up the old asylum and turn it into an apartment complex. However, in August of 2002, Rios was contacted by a group of Houston ghost hunters, Texoma Researchers Investigating Paranormal Phenomena (T.R.I.P.P.), who requested a visit to the property. They set up in the building, monitoring it for any signs of ghostly activity. The T.R.I.P.P.

group advised further that, according to *The Whichitan*, the Midwestern State University paper, a student at MSU told a group of high school friends that abandoned manacles were discovered in the asylum's basement. Haunted America Tours places it on their website as the fourth most haunted place list.

T.R.I.P.P. founder, Judy, replied to my query on the investigation by saying:

White Sanitarium is haunted. We had experiences there with something touching us. We picked up voices from entities (EVPs) and we got some interesting video. It is located on the corner of California Street and Olen Road. We have nicknamed it "Hotel

California." The song lyrics by the Eagles in their song "Hotel California," they sing the words "you can check out, but you can never leave." We feel that is what some of the patients did. In their minds they checked out, but they never left—even after their death.

We have the voices of several small children, and several adult voices. It was a combination sanitarium for ill people and an asylum for the mentally ill...

...We would lose power on our equipment when the activity would begin. In a bedroom upstairs, one night about six of us were sitting and talking, and the room became so cold that we actually had to leave the room. We had not experienced such an extreme in temperature change like that in our history of investigating.

One time there, we had a cameraman from a local TV station along with us to film a story the TV station was going to do on the asylum. Well, even though he was told by us ahead of time to bring extra batteries for his equipment, he failed to do so, and no sooner had he started filming and the activity began, his battery on his big camera was drained of its energy. He felt bad because he had been told. That same night we were downstairs in the main living area, and we were doing an EVP session, and we clearly heard a little girl's voice come from upstairs. The TV cameraman was a

skeptic, but he was the first to say he heard the voice, so they went upstairs to check it out and there was nothing there. A few days later, after the investigation, he wrote and told me that if he had not been there and experienced the things he did, he would still be a skeptic, but the experience changed the way he saw things now.

One of our team members felt something down by her foot and took a picture, and you can see in her picture where something was moving next to her foot.

The footage we have of all the anomalies going across the floors and around my hands are not explained. We have had several teams and others look at the videos to see if they could explain what we were seeing on the film, and no one could. We tested for bugs, anything that might fly, and nothing was found. We noticed too in one of the videos, that when one of the team members would move to check the camera, you could see that it appeared the anomalies would follow him.

The place has been a favorite haunt of this area for over forty years at least. You can ask most people who were raised in this town, and almost all of them have a story about the asylum.

It has been said that neighbors who live across the street have seen a female apparition walking out on the lawn sometimes at night. Others

have stated that sometimes at night, they could see what looked like a faint light on in the asylum, and some men sitting around a table playing cards. The area they were seen was the area used as a recreation room when it was open as an asylum.

There was a basement to the asylum, but once the current owners bought it, they filled in most of the basement. There is only a very small section that they left accessible. Downstairs as well as upstairs seem to have equal activity.

We picked up a young male entity stating that his name was not Michael. Not sure who called him that, but he wanted to make sure everyone knew that was not his name. There is a young female entity who was telling her grandmother that "he hurt me." Then there was an older female that called out to a male and it sounds like she called him Ronald.

We did find a large old knife right outside the area behind the asylum. Someone found what appeared to be some surgical instrument of some kind inside. There were still a few old books at the time. The place has been purchased and remodeled. The couple that owns it want to turn it into a bed and breakfast. Now, paranormal enthusiasts might enjoy staying there, but I feel that most people familiar with the place would not want to. We did not get a picture of an apparition, but we could feel them around us.

THE F.S. WHITE SANITARIUM
California and Olen Roads Wichita Falls, TX 76302

162

WHERE TO EAT

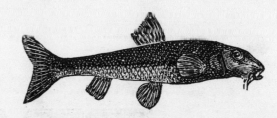

DEL FRISCO'S STEAKHOUSE

The Del Frisco's Steakhouse is located in the Galleria complex that formerly housed Lord and Taylor, in a hub of Houston's business and commercial action. It is an elegant two-story space with sweeping windows that offer guests a dramatic dining experience. In addition to a great menu, the steakhouse offers guests a little something extra with their New Orleans-inspired "Lagniappe" style. In the 1800s, it used to be a bathhouse, and a man was shot in the head here. Ghost historians claim his spirit roams the banquet halls and the upstairs bar.

DEL FRISCO'S STEAKHOUSE
5061 Westheimer Road, Suite 8060
Houston, TX 77056
Phone: (713) 355-2600
Email: delfriscos.houston@dfrg.com
Website: delfriscos.com

THE CATFISH PLANTATION

The Catfish Plantation in Waxahachie, Texas, has been featured on many national television shows and has been written about in varied publications for its apparent hauntings, as well as for its outstanding food.

The restaurant was founded in 1984 and sold to the current owners in 2007. Shortly after the place was founded as a restaurant, strange things began to occur. Items were moved from their original locations, and the owner came in one morning to find a fresh pot of coffee brewed for her already. There is a story of a fry basket levitating in the kitchen and the ghostly figure of a bride standing by a front window.

The place has been investigated by several paranormal groups over the years. In recent years, an investigation confirmed several spirits roaming the premises. Regardless of how many exist at the plantation, all are said to be friendly.

While the place is known for its other worldly inhabitants, they are also known for their outstanding food, prepared in a Creole way—obviously, the specialty of the house is catfish. So, while barbeque may be popular in Texas, there is nothing better than outstanding catfish and great ghost stories to go along with it. While there, ask to hear more haunting tales. The staff and owners will be more than happy to share.

You can also visit the restaurant's website, where you can not only learn about the menu, but also the many ghost stories of this fine Texas establishment.

THE CATFISH PLANTATION
814 Water Street, Waxahachie, TX 75165
Phone: (972) 937-9468
Website: http://www.catfishplantation.com

Brigham Young Farm House. Photograph courtesy Library of Congress

UTAH

WHERE TO VISIT

THE BRIGHAM YOUNG FARMHOUSE

The Brigham Young Farmhouse located in the historic Mormon district of Salt Lake City in the "Old Deseret Village," was constructed in the middle of the 1800s as part of a farm colony. It is considered to be haunted, with many reported paranormal events about the place.

The first haunting at the farmhouse is where people have claimed to have seen the spirit of Brigham Young in numerous places around the home. They have also communicated with a woman whose last name was Wilcox, who restored the home before giving it to the Mormon Church.

In the ballroom, there have been many instances documented by paranormal investigators who say they hear the voices of people talking and children playing and laughing. This was where, in the past, neighboring friends gathered to have parties, as well to provide a place for their children to play.

THE BRIGHAM YOUNG FARMHOUSE
2601 East Sunnyside Avenue (800 South), Salt Lake City, UT 84108
Phone: (801) 582-1847 Website: www.utah.com/stateparks/this_place.htm

THE
MCCUNE MANSION

The reportedly haunted McCune Mansion in Salt Lake City, Utah, is very popular among both residents of the city and tourists alike. It sits on a hill located near the downtown area of the city. This mansion was built in 1900 by wealthy entrepreneur Alfred W. McCune and his wife, Elizabeth, for half a million dollars. In 1901, the McCune family officially moved into the home, but when the couple's children grew up, they decided to move out and gave the mansion to the Mormon Church.

One of the hauntings said to occur in the McCune Mansion involves the spirit of a young girl, believed to be the same child pictured in a wall hanging in the home. She often is seen near a mirror on the West side of the mansion.

If you would like to take a tour of this haunted place, be sure to make reservations prior to your visit.

THE MCCUNE MANSION
200 North Main Street, Salt Lake City, UT 84103
Phone: (801) 531-8866 or (801) 533-3500
Website: http://www.mccunemansion.com/

Tours are given by the Utah Historical Society.

OLD TOOELE
HOSPITAL, ASYLUM 49

In 1873, Samuel F. Lee constructed the original building as a home for his family, but by 1913, the family moved out and the county turned it into a home for the elderly and those who required supervision, sort of an early nursing home, although many in the community had referred to it as the county poor house. In time, the county realized that the structure would make a good hospital.

The new hospital opened in 1953, and was originally known as the Toole Army Depot. A few minor adjustments were made to the building to make sure that the patients could be given proper medical care. Interestingly, there was no "morgue" for patients who died while in the structure, though there was one room designated for the dead to be placed until the local mortuary would pick up the body. When the mortuary was done with the remains, they were buried in the Tooele County Cemetery, which is beside the hospital.

The hospital is also the location for the filming of the movie *The Stand* by Stephen King. As an actual hospital, however, it was too outdated and it was officially closed in 2000.

The Utah Ghost Organization (UGO) conducted an investigation at the hospital in 2007. The group said they captured thousands of EVPs during their investigations, as well as videos with shadows and other unidentified things. The building is now used as a haunted attraction during the Halloween season that is referred to as "Asylum 49."

OLD TOOELE HOSPITAL, ASYLUM 49
140 East 200 South, Tooele, UT 84074
Phone: (435) 840-3709 Website: www.Asylum49.com

The Old Tooele Hospital offers ghosts hunts two times a
month from the beginning of the year to July.

VERMONT

WHERE TO VISIT

LAKE CHAMPLAIN

Champ is a legendary beast that roams the waters of Lake Champlain. Through the centuries there have been many alleged sightings of a creature that resembles an ancient plesiosaur, a dinosaur that became extinct millions of years ago. If what the people see is really that, then there could still be an ancient dinosaur swimming the waters of the mighty lake. It can be thought of as America's version of the Loch Ness Monster.

The city of Burlington has benefitted from Champ and utilizes it for tourism purposes. The city's minor league baseball team is actually called the Vermont Lake Monsters, and uses Champ as its mascot.

The beast was reportedly talked about by Native American tribes in the area. The first reported sighting actually occurred in 1883 when Sheriff Nathan H. Mooney claimed to have seen a giant water serpent. Since that time, there have been at least 300 documented sightings of the lake monster. It has been protected by both the New York and Vermont legislatures.

There is a monument dedicated to Champ on King Street Dock in Burlington, Vermont.

CHAMP MONUMENT
1 King Street, Burlington, VT 05041

EMILY'S BRIDGE

Emily's Bridge is probably the most famous covered bridge in the state of Vermont, called so because it is said to be haunted by the ghost of Emily. It's actual name is the Gold Brook Bridge. There are many stories about Emily and how she died on the bridge, but there is no historical evidence that she ever truly existed. Legend says that the name Emily came about from a high school student who wrote a paper about using a Ouija board on the bridge and an entity who answered claiming her name was Emily.

Regardless of who actually haunts the bridge, there have been many claims of paranormal activity there. Most of these events occur between the hours of 12 a.m. and 3:30 a.m. Strange noises are often heard on the bridge, such as footsteps, a rope tightening, or a girl screaming. People have reported scratches on their vehicles when they park on the bridge. Some claim to have been touched by Emily's ghost. Others have reported seeing a white apparition.

It might only be an urban legend, but *maybe* it is real. The only way to truly find out is by traveling across the bridge yourself.

EMILY'S BRIDGE
Gold Brook Road, Stowe, VT 05672
http://www.emilysbridge.com/

WHERE TO STAY

GOLDEN STAGE INN

The Golden Stage Inn Bed and Breakfast was a stagecoach inn, offering travelers a place to stay before Vermont became a state. The original part of the building was built in 1788, but most of the sprawling common rooms and bedrooms were added in the late 1800s. The hotel had been a stop on the Underground Railroad and has a long and colorful history.

The inn has two honeybee hives, as well as chicken and sheep living on the grounds, so if you love farm animals, this is a great place to stay.

Also, if you are a fan of ghosts, then the Golden State Inn will be of interest to you. At this haunted inn, the innkeepers have become so familiar seeing the young, friendly spirit, who appears dressed in a cloak and a large-brimmed hat, that they've actually named him George.

Also, being a bed and breakfast, you know you are going to enjoy at least one great meal a day!

GOLDEN STAGE INN
399 Depot Street, Okemo Valley, Proctorsville, VT 05153
Phone: (802) 226-7744 Email: goldenstageinn@tds.net Website: www.goldenstageinn.com

THE OLD STAGECOACH INN

The Old Stagecoach Inn was a very prominent place in Waterbury, back in the days when people traveled by horses. It was also during this time that there was a movement against the Masonic Orders. When the inn was opened, a local order of the Masonic Movement named "King David Lodge" used a back room of the Old Stagecoach Inn for secret meetings.

Up until 1848, this inn served as the main hotel for travelers, until the age of the railroads began, and bigger, fancier resorts opened. Eventually, a family by the name of "Henry" acquired the inn. This was a socially important family with a large amount of money and the Henry family wished to upgrade the look of the structure into a "modern Victorian" in order to make it more attractive to potential customers. Sylvester Henry had owned the land, but the most important member of the family in the history of the inn is Margaret Annette Henry. She is the central character for the history of the inn and was said to give it the appearance it has today.

Annette married Albert Spencer, who had made a fortune in rubber, and with the influx of millions of dollars into the family, Annette and her husband transformed the old farm into an edifice benefiting their new status in society. They made what were referred to as Queen Anne period alterations to the estate, including narrow clapboard sheathing, shingle clab gables, and a decoratively coursed chimney in the south side.

In 1907, Albert died and "Nettie," as she was called, was left a widow. She shut the inn down to the public and turned it into her home, where she lived most of her final years—until she was almost 100 years of age, and was placed in a nursing home until her death in 1947.

Once she died, her body was laid to rest in a mausoleum on the property. It is said that her spirit still haunts the Old Stagecoach Inn, and many claim that the spirit of Ms. Spencer seems to enjoy "spooking" people, making a rocking chair move, especially in room "2" where she'd slept.

If you are looking for interesting places to go in Vermont, be sure to stop and visit the Old Stagecoach Inn!

OLD STAGECOACH INN
18 N. Main Street, Waterbury, VT 05676
Phone: (802) 244-5056 Website: http://www.oldstagecoach.com/

THE EQUINOX HOTEL

One of the most popular stories of the Equinox Hotel surrounds the former President Abraham Lincoln and his family. In 1865, Lincoln's wife, Mary Todd Lincoln, decided to visit the hotel in Vermont.

Now, many employees have claimed to have seen the ghostly image of Mrs. Lincoln at the Equinox Hotel while cleaning on the third floor. As well, paranormal investigators have researched the structure, and say they have heard voices and felt a chill.

THE EQUINOX HOTEL
3567 Main Street, Route 7A
Manchester Village, VT
Phone: (800) 362-4747
Website: http://www.equinoxresort.com

VIRGINIA

★ ★ ★ WHERE TO VISIT ★ ★ ★

ABRAM'S DELIGHT

Abram's Delight was the domain of five generations of the prominent Hollingsworth family. It began with Abraham Hollingsworth, who came to the Commonwealth around 1728. He received a grant for 582 acres and originally built a log cabin on the land. Construction on the current house began in 1748. Abraham's son, Isaac (yes, the names sound a bit biblical), took over next. He was a leader of the local Quaker group and wanted to use the house for Quaker meetings. The house would continue to grow in size and stature.

Jonah Hollingsworth was the third generation of the family to reside here. He needed more space for his wife and thirteen children. Around 1800, they added the reception room. He had a portico added also (which is no longer standing).

Jonah's son, David, led the next generation to reside here. He was a successful businessman who was known as a community leader. He moved the stairway and also had a large lake constructed. A summer house was built on an island on the lake.

None of David's three children ever married and they inherited the property only two years before the Civil War began, probably not the best time to inherit a great estate in the South. Abram's Delight suffered damage, as did many other great properties of the time. Annie was the only one of the children to remain at the estate. Once she left, the house was left unoccupied for thirty years.

In 1943, the estate was purchased by the city of Winchester, who in turn preserved it as the oldest home in the city. The museum was opened in 1961.

I had the pleasure of touring Abram's Delight with my family a few years back, and it is a place I will never forget. I remember not only the majesty of the place, but also the absolute eeriness. You could tell that you were not alone. My mom asked the caretaker if there were any reported hauntings in the place, and we were told that yes, there appeared to be.

One of the most talked about ghost stories here is about Mary (also one of the children who inherited the estate), who died in the house in 1917. Mary lived an adventurous life for a woman of her time. She was a tall and masculine woman. She had disguised herself as a man for some time and drove a chuck wagon in the west during the Civil War. While in the war, it is said she was engaged to a woman, but returned home unmarried. The lady's family tracked Mary to her home and made her family (the Hollingsworths) pay restitution for deceiving the woman. When Mary died, Annie did not report her sister's death until the next day, so Mary's body laid in the house until that time. Because of this, the spirit is said to remain there today.

There are many stories of Mary haunting this great estate. The best way to learn about them is to tour the great building and ask questions.

ABRAM'S DELIGHT
1340 S. Pleasant Valley Road, Winchester, VA 22601
Phone: (540) 662-6519 Website: http://www.winchesterhistory.org/abrams_delight.htm

WASHINGTON

★ ★ ★ WHERE TO VISIT ★ ★ ★

BILLY SPEIDEL'S UNDERGROUND TOUR

Seattle has another world beneath its bustling streets: Billy Speidel's Underground. Filled with subterranean passages, storefronts, and the ghosts of times past, this tour takes you along the old roads of Seattle, as guides tell you the stories of pioneers and the history of a great city. According to their website: "It's history with a twist!"

Seattle had been consumed by the Great Fire of 1889. After the fire, which destroyed twenty-five square blocks of mostly wooden buildings in the center of Seattle, the city decided that all new construction had to be of stone or brick masonry. The city also decided to rise above its old level, which brought about the underground. The city built retaining walls, eight feet or higher, on either side of the old streets, had the space between the walls filled in and paved over to effectively raise the streets, making them one story higher than the old streets had been.

The tour has been recognized on many television shows, bringing people in touch with the city's fascinating past.

There are those who have discussed seeing people dressed in period clothing in the Seattle Underground. With the history of the area, there is no reason to think that it is not haunted. As you walk along the streets, you may hear or even see things that you never expected. Regardless, it is certainly a macabre tour.

BILLY SPEIDEL'S UNDERGROUND TOUR
608 First Avenue, Seattle, WA 98104
Phone: (206) 682 4646 Website: http://www.undergroundtour.com/

Seattle's Pioneer Square, between Cherry Street and Yesler Way. Take the James Street Exit from Interstate 5.

WHERE TO EAT

BILLY'S BAR & GRILL

Whenever I visit Aberdeen, I feel that I am being transported into the television show *Twin Peaks*, with the beautiful scenery and the colorful people. Aberdeen is most famous for being the home of Nirvana legend Kirk Cobain, and that is reason enough to visit this amazing city. But there is another great reason to go, and that is to have dinner at Billy's Bar and Grill.

Billy's is named for a Billy, who did in fact exist in Aberdeen. Billy had been an admired secretary of the local sailor's union headquarters that was above the Grand Saloon. But eventually, Billy began to make up his own rules that served his own interests. Soon, there were robberies, shootings, and arsons that were traced to him. After a trial, he was sent to prison where he was said to be a model prisoner.

One of the occurrences that is most discussed is that Billy's soul has returned. Shot glasses and mugs are said to fly off the wall, smashing into the bar at the opposite wall. Items are also said to jump off the shelves in the kitchen, then crash to the floor. Some think this is Billy throwing a fit.

Others have seen apparitions, both upstairs and down. Some are said to be the ghosts of the late prostitutes who used to work the building in years past.

BILLY'S BAR AND GRILL
Heron and G Street, Aberdeen, Washington 98520
Phone: (360) 533-7144 Website: https://www.facebook.com/BillysBarAndGrill

WHERE TO STAY

★ ★ ★   ★ ★ ★

THORNEWOOD CASTLE

Thornewood Castle is a 500-year-old Tudor Gothic, taken from England in pieces and brought to the Pacific Northwest. These pieces were used to completely rebuild the castle and it is now a historic site, as well as famous hotel—and, it's rumored to be haunted. The many people who have worked, visited, and researched Thornewood have claimed to encounter ghosts as they toured the castle.

Individuals who have visited or stayed at this beautiful haunted castle have claimed that it is quite a unique experience. Thornewood was the setting for an ABC Stephen King mini-series airing in 2002, called *Rose Red*. Filming for the movie took place for six months there in 2000. The DVD of the movie is available at the Castle.

This is a private residence and located in a private neighborhood. It can only be seen when coming for previously-reserved overnight lodging or as a scheduled event, such as a wedding or corporate rental.

THORNEWOOD CASTLE
8601 North Thorne Lane SW, Tacoma, WA 98498
Phone: (253) 584-4393 Email: info@thornewoodcastle.com
Website: www.thornewoodcastle.com

THE HARVARD EXIT THEATER

In the 1920s, this place was known as the "Women's Century Club" and was a home for club members until 1968. The theater is known to show art and foreign films, and is also the home of film festivals, such as the Seattle International Film Festival.

As word began to spread that the structure was haunted, newspapers, television programs, authors, photographers, and even paranormal investigators have traveled in search of evidence and stories about it.

One of the stories revolves around a murder in the area where the theater now stands. The ghost is known as Peter and is described as being a portly man, who you are able to see through. He is said to wear an old-fashioned suit and is known for his sense of humor.

Also, in the balcony of the first floor, there is said to be an apparition of a woman, but that is not the only female spirit who is said to roam the premises. Bertha Landis is perhaps the most famous spirit at the theater, as she has been the most seen by visitors.

Visit the theater and maybe you will have a chance to be greeted by one of the spirits.

THE HARVARD EXIT THEATER
807 East Roy at Harvard, Seattle, WA 98102
Phone: (206) 781-5755
Website: www.landmarktheatres.com/
market/seattle/harvardexittheatre.htm

WASHINGTON, D.C.

WHERE TO VISIT

FORD THEATER

Everyone is familiar with the historic Ford Theater and its place in our country's history.

Abraham Lincoln, considered our nation's finest president, was visiting the theater with his wife, Mary Todd Lincoln, to see a performance of *Our American Cousin* only five days after Robert E. Lee surrendered at Appomattox Courthouse ending the war.

The famous thespian, John Wilkes Booth, had made his way to the Lincolns' box seats and shot the president before sneaking out of the back of the theater, thus ending the life of one of our nation's greatest men.

The theater was originally a house of worship for the First Baptist Church of Washington, before the church moved to a newly built structure.

John T. Ford bought the building and turned it into a theater. It was destroyed by a fire in 1862, but was quickly rebuilt and the new theater opened in August of 1863, becoming one of the finest theaters in the area.

After Lincoln was killed, the government paid Ford $100,000 and it ceased to be used as a theater. It was taken over by the military in the late 1800s, and served as a facility for the War Department.

The front part of the building collapsed in 1893, killing 22 clerks and injuring many others. The building was repaired, but turned into a government warehouse until 1911, and then was unused for many years.

A bill was passed in 1955 to prepare an engineering study for the reconstruction of the building. In 1964, Congress approved funds to restore the historic building and the theatre was finally reopened in January 30, 1968.

The Ford's Theatre Museum and Center for Education and Leadership offers exhibits and artifacts related to President Lincoln that deal with his presidency as well as his assassination and his legacy.

There have been a few witnesses over the years who say that a haunting of Lincoln's assassination repeats itself at times. They say that there are footsteps heard rushing towards the box where the president and his wife sat, followed by a gunshot and screams.

There is also said to be an icy presence on a specific part of the stage by various actors who feel it is the ghost of Booth himself. Some have been said to have seen his spirit running across the stage.

While most reports of Abraham Lincoln's ghost are said to happen in the White House, some have claimed to have seen his spirit here, too.

Regardless if you are hoping to see a haunt, or just a show, or even to visit the scene of one of the most important and sad events in American history, this theater is a must-see during your visit to the national capital.

FORD THEATER
511 10th Street NW, Washington, D.C. 20004
Phone: (202) 347-4833 Website: http://www.fordstheatre.org/

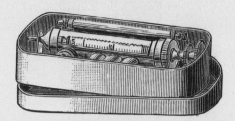

NATIONAL MUSEUM OF CRIME & PUNISHMENT

Unlike many museums in the District of Columbia, the National Museum of Crime and Punishment is a for-profit institution that was established in 2008 by businessman Joe Morgan in partnership with Joe Walsh of *America's Most Wanted* television series.

There are more than 700 artifacts that relate to the history of crime and its consequences in our country, as well as in popular culture. Here you will find exhibits on colonial crime, pirates, outlaws of the old west, mob-related items, mass murderers, and white collar criminals. The museum includes a mock police station with a booking room, celebrity mug shots, lie detector tests, as well as a capital punishment room with an electric chair, a lethal injection machine, and re-creations of a gas chamber and a guillotine. Visitors to the museum are guided though the process of solving crimes with forensic science techniques.

At one time, the museum was also home to the studios of the popular and long-running television show *America's Most Wanted*.

NATIONAL MUSEUM OF CRIME AND PUNISHMENT
575 7th St. NW, Washington, D.C. 20004
Phone: (202) 621-5550 Website: www.crimemuseum.org

During the Halloween season, the popular museum hosts what is referred to as
"Fright Nights at the Museum." This haunted house is very popular in the D.C. area.

WHERE TO STAY

OMNI SHOREHAM HOTEL

A strange presence is said to lurk in Suite 870 of the Omni Shoreham Hotel in our national capital—that of a ghost.

While the room has an amazing view and a penthouse terrace, the reality is that you may not be spending your night alone. Some of the things that are said to take place, in what is commonly referred to as the ghost suite, are faint voices in empty rooms, televisions and lights turning on and off on their own, and cold breezes.

During the early years of the hotel, three people were said to have died unexpectedly in the suite. At the time, it was an apartment that was occupied by the hotel's owner and family. One night, the live-in housekeeper of the family dropped dead while calling the hotel's front desk. The owner's daughter and wife also were said to have died mysteriously in the suite, and the owner moved out shortly thereafter. The suite remained abandoned for about fifty years.

Even when the suite was vacant, there were said to be things going on. There were claims of doors slamming shut and furniture that moved on its own. Those who were staying in the adjoining room would call and complain of noises coming from the suite.

When the hotel was sold in the 1980s, the suite was renovated, but to this day it is seldom rented out, and not to the public—mostly to house dignitaries and guests of the hotel.

Even if you are unable to stay in the haunted room, perhaps you can stay in one that is adjoining and still hear the noises that so many, over the years, have been complaining about.

OMNI SHOREHAM HOTEL
2500 Calvert Street, Washington, D.C. 20008 Phone: (202) 234-0700
Website: http://www.omnihotels.com/FindAHotel/WashingtonDCShoreham.aspx

WEST VIRGINIA

WHERE TO VISIT

MOUNDSVILLE STATE PENITENTIARY

West Virginia Penitentiary, otherwise called Moundsville, opened in 1876, with a striking stone facade and Gothic architecture. According to popular legend, Moundsville was built on an old Native American burial ground. Constructed to hold only 480 prisoners, by the early 1930s, it housed over 2,000, by fitting three to four in a single cell. Moundsville took over all executions for the state. In all, 94 men were either hung or electrocuted. The executions, however, were only a small part of the violent past at Moundsville. Suicide, inmate against inmate killings, and violent punishments caused the deaths of hundreds of inmates here.

The following are excerpts from a former superintendent's interview after he resigned from the prison, describing the atrocities and exposing the violence and torture on inmates by prison officials. Those accounts, such as the use of a device called "The Kicking Jenny," are as follows:

It [The Kicking Jenny] is an instrument invented and built in the prison. It is made somewhat in the shape of a quarter-circle, with the highest end about three or four feet above the platform upon which it is set. The prisoner is stripped naked and bent over upon the machine. His feet are fastened to the floor with ropes, while his hands, which are stretched over the upper end, are tied with roped attached to small blocks, by which a tension so strong that the frame of the prisoner can almost be torn in two can be made with a slight pull. After the prisoner is placed in position, the Superinten-dent, or whoever does the whipping, takes a heavy whip, made of sole leather, two pieces of which, about three feet long, are sewn together and the ends scraped slightly round-ing, the lash being three inches broad at the handle, tapering to a point. With the whip, the prisoner is beaten until he is almost dead, or the strength of the man who is doing the whipping gives out.

The shoo-fly was an instrument so arranged that the victim could be placed with his feet in the stocks, his arms pinioned, and his head fastened so that he could not move it. Then someone would take the hose and turn the water full upon the prisoner's face—this until the victim was partly strangled to death, an early form of water boarding.

The circular entrance gate which was used to separate ar-riving inmates from the warden's living quarters is a source of ghost stories. According to reports of visitors over the years, the circular cage turns periodically by itself, as if ghostly inmates are condemned to return again and again.

Another chilling aspect of crime and history is that Charles Manson is said to have served time at Moundsville and wrote to the warden on different occasions asking to be transferred back to the facility. However, in the year 1986, the West Virginia Supreme Court ruled the small cells were cruel and unusual punishment and ordered the facility closed.

Trans Allegheny lunatic asylum.
Photograph courtesy of Chandra Lampriech

Trans Allegheny
lunatic asylum.
*Photograph courtesy of
Chandra Lampriech*

TRANS-ALLEGHENY LUNATIC ASYLUM

Construction on this massive structure started in Weston, West Virginia, in 1858, using prison labor, and eventually, skilled European stonemasons to complete it. During the Civil War, construction was interrupted for almost a year. Patients started arriving in 1864, although the structure was not completely finished until 1881. This enormous 242,000-square-foot building was built on over 650 acres, and was originally meant to house 250 patients, but by 1950, it held over 2,400. The hospital was renamed Weston State Hospital in 1913.

Records indicate frequent assaults and worse, as patients killed other patients, female employees were violated, and a nurse went missing for nearly two months and was later found dead at the bottom of a never-used stairway. Visitors have reported the sounds of gurneys being pushed up and down the hallways, and in the electroshock treatment rooms, people say they hear faint screams. Voices can be heard and apparitions seen all around the facility, with the majority of it occurring actively on the fourth floor, which was the Civil War wing.

Eighty years passed until, in 1990, the hospital was designated a historical landmark. In 2007, it was bought during an auction and is now open for tours, after the new owners officially changed the name back to its original name, The Trans-Allegheny Lunatic Asylum. It was a year later when the television show *Ghost Hunters* with the TAPS team was invited in to investigate for paranormal evidence. They said they heard a female laugh, banging noises, and Grant Wilson of the show claimed there was an apparition standing in a corner that was "being sucked out of the room."

TRANS ALLEGHENY LUNATIC ASYLUM
71 Asylum Drive, Weston, WV 26452 Phone: (304) 269-5070
Website: http://trans-alleghenylunaticasylum.com/

The historic location offers history and ghost tours. Monday, by appointment only, Tuesday, Wednesday, Thursday, and Sunday, 12 p.m. to 6 p.m. Friday 12 p.m. to 6 p.m. and Saturday 10 a.m. to 6 p.m. If you are interested in a private paranormal or historic tour (daytime), please call.

Mothman Museum.
*Photograph courtesy of the
Mothman Museum*

Mothman Museum. *Photograph courtesy of the Mothman Museum*

Mothman Museum. *Photograph courtesy of the Mothman Museum*

MOTHMAN MUSEUM

If you are truly excited by going to unusual places, then be sure to visit the Mothman Museum in Point Pleasant, West Virginia. The museum is the only one of its kind in the world, dedicated to the famous Mothman.

Here you will see the largest collection of props and memorabilia from the movie *The Mothman Prophecies*, as the sightings and encounters that the movie details actually took place in Point Pleasant. The museum discusses the impact the phenomenon has had on the community.

There is also a Mothman Tour that originates at the museum and will take you around to the different sites related to the famous Mothman.

MOTHMAN MUSEUM
411 Main Street, Point Pleasant, WV 25550
Phone: (304) 812-5211 Website: http://www.mothmanmuseum.com/

Mothman Museum.
*Photograph courtesy of the
Mothman Museum*

WHERE TO STAY

THE LOWE HOTEL

The Lowe Hotel is not only reported to be haunted, but seems to also have ties to the famous Mothman. A newspaper article at the front desk tells not only about the hotel hauntings, but about the sightings of the famous Mothman in Point Pleasant.

This historic hotel is located in the center of the Point Pleasant Historic District. It was built in 1901 with the original name of the Spencer Hotel and was later renamed. Purchased by Ruth and Rush Finley in 1990, it has been continually upgraded. The place is said to be extremely friendly and a great experience for the traveler.

The third floor is said to be haunted by a small child on a tricycle. Sometimes the spirit is seen, and other times you just hear the child's laugh or the squeaking of a tricycle. This floor is said to be the most actively haunted with a man in 1930s-style clothing rumored to be seen in room 314. Many claim to hear the sounds of a string quartet playing in the fourth-floor ballroom day or night. Also, in the mezzanine, between the first and second floors, there is rumored to be the famous ghost of a disheveled young woman who is seen barefoot in a nightgown dancing.

While staying at the hotel, be sure to visit The Red Parrot Café. Maybe you can hear the locals tell tales of the famous Mothman.

THE LOWE HOTEL
401 Main Street, Point Pleasant, WV 25550
Phone: (304) 675-2260 Website: http://www.thelowehotel.com/

WISCONSIN

WHERE TO VISIT

★ ★ ★ ★ ★ ★ ★ ★

RIPLEY'S
BELIEVE IT OR NOT ODDITORIUM

Awhile ago, I happened to drive through Wisconsin Dells and came across the Ripley's museum there.

There are some great exhibits, but the thing I remember most vividly is the rope bridge that took me over the crash of a plane. I felt like Indiana Jones on one of his adventures crossing it.

There are two floors and eight great exhibits. The one that seems to really get people's attention is the King Tut display. There are many great illusions, as you would expect at a Ripley's attraction. I always find myself trying to read each and every display, even those in the restrooms.

RIPLEY'S BELIEVE IT OR NOT ODDITORIUM
115 Broadway, Wisconsin Dells, WI 53965
Phone: (608) 254-2184 Website: www.ripleys.com

Ripley's Wisconsin is open the following times and months: September: 10 a.m. to 8 p.m. Sunday to Thursday, 10 a.m. to 10 p.m. Friday to Saturday; October: 10 a.m. to 6 p.m. Sunday to Thursday, 10 a.m. to 8 p.m. Friday to Saturday; November to February: 10 a.m. to 5 p.m. Friday to Monday, Closed Tuesday to Thursday; March 1 to March 22: 10 a.m. to 5 p.m. Sunday to Thursday, 10 a.m. to 6 p.m. Friday to Saturday; March 23 to April 15: 10 a.m. to 8 p.m. Daily; April 16 to May 24: 10 a.m. to 5 p.m. Sunday to Thursday, 10 a.m. to 8 p.m. Friday to Saturday. General admission (12 and up) $12.99 Children (5-11) $10.99, tots (4 and under) FREE with paying adult.

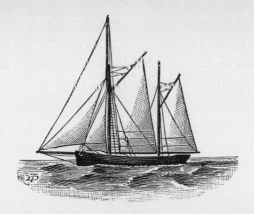

DELLS LOST VOYAGE

I always enjoy a good murder mystery show, but have never heard of one held on a boat before—not until now.

The Lost Voyage is an hour-and-a-half-long expedition that leaves its berth at 8:30 p.m. every night, traveling up the Wisconsin River. Passengers disembark to continue on foot through Cold Water Canyon. During this first half, travelers will be solving riddles by way of various discoveries of clues. On the way back, visitors are told the story of the *Badger*, a tour boat that was caught up in a vicious storm back in 1943 that disappeared...until now. The *Badger* mysteriously was discovered by a group of teenagers who captured it on tape in Cold Water Canyon – and the youths themselves are now nowhere to be found!

It is up to the participants to crack the case! Eager detectives can get an early start by visiting www.dellslostvoyage.com/solve. Here you can find clues and a list of questions, the answers to some of which can be found online as well. The Lost Voyage provides the rest, as answers are given throughout the tour. Once you think you've solved the case, head back online and submit your prospective code to be eligible for amazing prizes. Feeling confident? Come back year after year and attempt to solve the case anew, as there will be different questions and clues every summer.

So, if you are looking for something completely different, visit the Wisconsin Dells and take a mystery trip you won't soon forget.

DELLS LOST VOYAGE
11 Broadway, Wisconsin Dells, WI 53965
Phone: (608) 254-8555 Website: http://www.dellslostvoyage.com/HOME.html

WHERE TO STAY

HISTORIC BRUMDER MANSION BED & BREAKFAST

Constructed in 1910 by George Brumder, in the architectural designs of both Gothic and Victorian style, this particular establishment is considered to be one of the best paranormal spots in all of Wisconsin. The bed and breakfast stands four stories high and has a square footage of 8,000. The Brumder Mansion was purchased by a lady named Carol some time later, and she bought many old antiques for the place. The building is filled with old dolls, furniture, art, and other interesting objects.

It has been established that there are at least three ghostly spirits in the mansion, after an investigation conducted by a team called The North Alliance of Paranormal Investigators. Visitors and employees have heard unexplained voices, especially that of an old lady who is said to haunt the place. A psychic was brought in and determined her name was Susan, found in what is referred to as the "Gold Room." Another spirit can be occasionally seen in the suite where George Brumder himself lived.

If you will be in the area, check it out. Call ahead and make reservations, as you will certainly enjoy your stay.

HISTORIC BRUMDER MANSION BED AND BREAKFAST
3046 West Wisconsin Avenue, Milwaukee, WI 53208
Phone: (414) 342-9767 Website: http://milwaukeebedbreakfast.com/

WHERE TO EAT

FLYNN'S STEAK HOUSE

Most everybody loves a good steak. I personally, to no surprise of my readers, like mine blue rare, that is as rare as possible. That always leaves a little blood to soak my baked potato in. Along with a glass or four of Merlot, it can be the end of a perfect evening.

A great place to have an amazing steak, while in the presence of ghosts, is Flynn's Steak House.

Flynn's was built in 1868. It was originally known as the "Young House" for a period of time and then the "Harris House" before finally arriving at the name Flynn's Steak House.

There are hotel rooms located on the upper floor of Flynn's Steak House, although they no longer function as hotel rooms. Regardless, this history plays a role in the hauntings that are said to occur at the establishment. Some area locals have said that a girl by the name of Mary died in a fire in the mid-1860s in one of the rooms while trying to light a kerosene lantern, and that her spirit still haunts the premises.

Patrons at the restaurant have reported objects moving without any real explanation. Strange noises and disembodied voices have also been reported. A manager arrived one morning to find a flannel table cloth, a type that is not used in the restaurant, on one of the tables.

Candles are said to light themselves and gas burners turn themselves on without reason. There are reports that a woman in white who wears old-fashioned clothing has been seen in the restaurant. Many of the locals believe the stories are due to the history of this establishment, and if it is good enough for the locals, it is good enough for us.

FLYNN'S STEAK HOUSE
1101 1st Center Avenue, Brodhead, WI 53520-1423
Phone: (608) 897-2626 Website: https://www.facebook.com/pages/Flynn-Steak-House/118111894871044

WYOMING

WHERE TO VISIT

FT. BRIDGER STATE HISTORIC SITE

Fort Bridger was established by Jim Bridger and Louis Vasquez, in 1843, as a supply stop for those who were emigrating to the area. It was obtained by Mormons who came to the area in the 1850s and later became a military outpost in 1858. In 1933, it was dedicated as a Wyoming Historical Landmark and Museum.

Several of the buildings have been restored from the military time period, as well as a reconstructed trading post that had been operated by Mr. Bridger, and an interpretive archaeological site that contains the base of the cobble rock wall that was built by the Mormons. A museum contains artifacts from all the important historical periods of the site.

It is said that there are ghosts in almost every historic structure on the premises. There is supposedly a ghost of a dog that was decorated for heroism for saving the life of a young child. One of the ghosts in the museum is said to enjoy playing with the copier located there. It is thought that most of the spirits are of soldiers who were stationed at the fort in the mid to late 1800s. Regardless, the ghost are thought to be harmless, so you shouldn't have any problems with them while visiting.

FT. BRIDGER STATE HISTORIC SITE
136 Carter Avenue, P.O. Box 112, Fort Bridger, WY 82933
Phone: (307) 782-3842 Website: http://wyoparks.state.wy.us/Site/SiteInfo.aspx?siteID=17

Fort Bridger State Historic Site can be reached by taking Interstate 80, Exit 34; then approximately three miles to the town of Ft. Bridger. The site is on the south side of the highway located behind the bronze statue of Jim Bridger. Site Grounds Hours: open 8 a.m. to dark – April 1 to October. 31. There are no services during the winter. Museum hours: open 8:30 a.m. to 5 p.m. May 1 to September 30, open weekends 9 a.m. to 4:30 p.m. in April and October.

WYOMING
FRONTIER PRISON MUSEUM

During the Wyoming Frontier Prison's 80 years of operation, 13,500 inmates were kept at the facility. Towering into the night skyline, the concrete is crumbling, paint is peeling off the ceilings... As tourists come to visit, they can almost hear the clanging metal doors shut behind them.

In its past, guards would drag misbehaving inmates to a small, concrete-walled room that had a cement pole known as the Punishment Pole that ran from the floor to ceiling. They would chain inmates to it and whip them with rubber hoses or leather straps until they screamed, so that all of the other prisoners in A Block would hear them.

This is one of the only prisons we are aware of that allows visitors to sit in a real gas chamber, on the very same steel seat as five executed prisoners.

Another form of execution used by the prison was a unique "humane gallows," a device that had the condemned prisoner essentially hanging over a trap door that fell open when their body weight forced water out of counterbalanced bucket. The condemned could hear the water draining out the entire time, and this gave them time to think about what they'd done.

Kaitlyn, who has been giving tours at the prison since she was 15, says that inmates used to "...put razors into the soap. They would break the light bulbs and put shards of glass in other people's food."

Up a long flight of stairs is what is known as "The Death House" where the condemned were forced to stay, awaiting their executions. In the corner is a gas chamber, which is made from a steel tank with thick windows and an air pump that forced the gas inside.

The Wyoming Frontier Prison has a small museum next to its gift shop, which includes a doll-sized working model of the humane gallows, and a mounted display of rope samples from every successful hanging.

THE WYOMING FRONTIER PRISON
500 W. Walnut Street, Rawlins, WY 82301
Phone: (307) 324-4422 Website: http://www.wyomingfrontierprison.org/

If you would like to visit the prison, you may do so during the months of April through October from 8:30 a.m. to 6:30 p.m., and in November through March, 9 a.m. to 5 p.m. Monday to Friday.

WHERE TO STAY

IVY HOUSE INN
BED & BREAKFAST

If you are looking for a place to stay while visiting Casper, look no further than the Ivy House Inn Bed and Breakfast. This place is appealing since it is not only haunted by the ghost of its prior owner, but by her two cats as well. Being a cat lover myself, I have always been fascinated by the concept of any ghost pet, especially that of a cat.

The Cape Cod-style building was built in 1916 by a couple with the last name of White. The three-story dwelling was completed in 1940 when two grand front porches were added.

The story is that Mrs. White was a very controlling person. Allegedly, she now continues in her old ways as a ghost, making sure that guests do not smoke or drink at the inn. That being said, she is supposedly around the inn all of the time, according to the owners and the guests who stay.

It is said her face will appear in windows and in mirrors, which could certainly cause a fright. Her shadowy figure is many times seen walking down the halls and even through the walls. Her image has also been said to have shown up in photos taken by those who have stayed there.

Guests have seen two Siamese cats roaming through the inn, while others say that there was a cat sleeping with them, happily purring. Some who have stayed here have claimed to have seen a gentleman in the parking area…could this be the late Mr. White?

So, while you are in Casper, be sure to stay at a place where not only humans haunt the premises, but also two very sweet cats.

IVY HOUSE INN BED AND BREAKFAST
815 South Ash, Casper, Wyoming 82601
Phone: (307) 265-0974 Website: http://www.ivyhouseinn.com

★ ★ ★   ★ ★ ★

THE
WONDER BAR

The Wonder Bar has been a popular Casper landmark for decades. Al Swanson, the proprietor in 1942, allowed cowboys to ride up to the bar and buy beer for both rider and mount. Both would ride out the back door to the alley, which is an amazing image to cross your mind when you are in the heart of cowboy country.

The establishment has not only a great menu, but a great selection of beers, including micro-brews that are made on the premises. That being said, those are not the only spirits that you will find at the bar.

All ghost hunters have been looking for the holy grail, a full body apparition, and there have been reports of one that has been found on the stairs at The Wonder Bar. There are also reports that lights turn off and on without any way to explain it, as well as disembodied sounds.

THE WONDER BAR
256 South Center Street, Casper, WY 82601
Phone: (307) 234-4110 Website: http://www.thewonderbar.com/

HAWAII

WHERE TO VISIT

BONEYARDS OF OAHU

The ancient tradition of the Hawaiian people was to put their dead in unmarked private graves, with the location known only to the family.

On the island of Honolulu, in Manoa, somewhat north of the University of Hawaii campus on old Manoa Road, there lies a small neglected cemetery, which is now part of the front yard of the Manoa Valley Theatre. This spot is the final resting place for some of the island's oldest non-Hawaiian residents, of Chinese, Hawaiian, Portuguese, and Spanish descent of the island.

This boneyard is a mass gravesite, otherwise called a hecatomb, which is an ancient type of burial, once common throughout Europe, and it was closed by the Honolulu Board of Health in the 1930s. At the rear of the cemetery is an abandoned mausoleum with the remains still visible inside.

The majority of graves in this area are that of Chinese immigrants from the 1920s, and most show no trace of any markers; those that remain are very weathered. This necropolis has many ceramic urns used to store human bones, stacked on wood planks. The earliest dates on those few graves that can be seen are from the 1950s. It is a somber place in the middle of a tropical paradise.

Even in the land of sunshine, Hawaii, there is a place for the Gothic tourist to visit.

★ ★ ★ AFTERWORD ★ ★ ★

This book was written for our friends, our fans and all the many people who took their time in speaking to us during the completion of this book.

Writing this volume was an intense labor of love, and many long were hours spent pouring over our research to locate information on just the perfect places without being repetitive—it was a challenge.

We knew in advance we did not want it to simply be a "most haunted" multi-state book, but rather for it to be one that at every turn of the page you would be mesmerized and surprised by what you found, just as much as we were in locating all of it in the first place.

Looking back on all the states we have personally been to or researched has made for an exciting and educational experience unlike any before in our lives. We hope you have not only enjoyed the experience with us, but will make good use of the information on the locations and visitor information listed in these pages and follow in our footsteps. Perhaps as you join us in doing more than just reading about these macabre places, you will seek as many of them as possible, firsthand for yourself. Who knows? We just may cross paths with you in the process.

IN ANY CASE, WE WISH SAFE AND SCARY JOURNEYS TO YOU.

E.R. VERNOR (CORVIS NOCTURNUM)

KEVIN EADS

THE WORLD IS A BOOK AND THOSE WHO DO NOT TRAVEL READ ONLY ONE PAGE.

—St. Augustine